THE ULTIMATE
NBT GUIDE

300 PRACTICE QUESTIONS

LIZZY COLE
DR. ROHAN AGARWAL

UniAdmissions

ISBN 978-1-912557-74-5

Published by *RAR Medical Services Limited*
www.uniadmissions.co.uk
info@uniadmissions.co.uk
Tel: +44 (0) 208 068 0438

ABOUT THE AUTHORS

Rohan is the **Director of Operations** at *UniAdmissions* and is responsible for its technical and commercial arms. He graduated from Gonville and Caius College, Cambridge in Natural Sciences and is a fully qualified doctor. Over the last five years, he has tutored hundreds of successful Oxbridge and Medical applicants. He has also authored ten books on admissions tests and interviews.

Rohan has taught Physiology to undergraduates and interviewed medical school applicants for Cambridge. He has published research on bone physiology and writes education articles for the Independent and Huffington Post. In his spare time, Rohan enjoys playing the piano and table tennis.

Lizzy was the first in her family to go to university, graduating with a degree in Natural Sciences from the University of Cambridge in 2011. She subsequently trained as a teacher at Hughes Hall College, Cambridge and won a scholarship to study a PhD at the University of St Andrews. Since then, she has taught at the University of Cambridge and become an experienced private tutor, as well as authored countless blogs and articles on the university admissions process. She has a passion for health and fitness; in her spare time Lizzy enjoys cooking, playing softball and runs her own nutrition practice.

CONTENTS

THE BASICS

What is the **NBT?**
The National Benchmark Test (NBT) is used by universities in South Africa to make admissions decisions and to assess academic readiness.

What does the **NBT** consist of?
The NBT is multiple choice, where answers are recorded on a 'bubble sheet'. These answer sheets are scanned and then translated into scores.

There are two tests. The Academic Literacy and Quantitative Literacy test (AQL) are combined into one multiple-choice test, which is a total of three hours. The AQL test is written by applicants to all programmes. The second test is Mathematics (MAT), which is written by applicants to programmes for which mathematics is a requirement. The MAT test is also multiple-choice, with three hours allowed. Both tests are taken on the same day; the AQL in the morning and MAT in the afternoon.

Test	Timing	Topics Tested	Questions	Calculator
AQL	3 hours	Academic Literacy Quantitative Literacy	MCQs	Not Allowed
MAT (for those taking Mathematical and Science subjects only)	3 hours	Mathematics	MCQs	Not Allowed

What do I need to revise for the **NBT?**
The NBT tests the following areas of knowledge. Revising these in general, alongside working through the questions in this book, is a great way to feel confident and well prepared ahead of the exam.

Academic Literacy

- Make meaning from academic text.
- Understand vocabulary related to academic study.
- Evaluate evidence used to support claims made by writers.
- Extrapolate and draw inferences and conclusions from text.
- Differentiate main idea from supporting ideas in the overall and specific organisation of a passage.
- Identify text differences as related to the writers' purposes, audiences, and forms of communication.
- Understand how syntax and punctuation are used to express meaning; and
- Understand basic numerical concepts used in text.

Quantitative Literacy

- Apply quantitative procedures and reasoning in symbolic and non-symbolic situations.
- Apply information from a variety of tables, graphs, charts and text.
- Integrate information obtained from multiple sources.
- Perform multiple-step calculations using information presented with text, symbols, and graphs.
- Identify trends and patterns in various situations.
- Apply properties of simple geometric shapes to determine measurements; and
- Interpret quantitative information presented verbally, symbolically, and graphically.

Mathematics

- Understand and apply properties of the real number system, including surds and exponents.
- Recognise and use patterns, including sequences and series.
- Apply relationships such as ratios and percentages in a variety of contexts.
- Apply the results of algebraic manipulations with equations and inequalities.
- Understand the function concept and identify properties of functions
- Interpret transformations of functions represented algebraically or graphically.

- Identify relationships between graphs and their equations, or inequalities and the regions they describe.
- Apply trigonometric identities and concepts in solving problems.
- Understand properties and interpret representations of two-dimensional and three-dimensional shapes.
- Apply principles of analytic geometry.
- Interpret various representations and measures of data; and
- Use logical skills in making deductions and determining the validity of given assertions.

Why is the NBT used?

Competition for places at top South African universities tends to be fierce, meaning that the universities must use the NBT to help differentiate between applicants.

When do I sit the NBT?

You can sit the NBT from May onwards and only need to write the test once, even if you are applying to more than one university. You should write the NBT when you feel ready. However, you must meet the closing dates and deadlines for the institutions where you are applying.

What language may I use to write the NBT?

The NBT is available in English and Afrikaans. When registering, you will be asked to indicate the language in which you wish to write. You can only choose one language; there is no option to write one test in English and the other in Afrikaans.

How much does the NBT cost to sit?

The Academic and Quantitative Literacy (AQL) test costs R100.00 on its own, while both the Academic and Quantitative Literacy (AQL) and Mathematics (MAT) tests together cost R200.00.

Can I resit the NBT?

Students can choose to attempt the test twice during the same cycle, but the second result is not accepted by any of the leading universities.

What do I need to bring with me?

You must bring:

- Your South African ID booklet, foreign passport or a birth certificate with an affidavit from the police including a recent photograph.
- Pencils and eraser
- Water and lunch, if you are writing both the AQL and MAT

Do not bring a calculator, ruler, dictionary or other learning aid.

How do I get my test results?

Approximately two to four weeks after you have written the tests, you may access your results on the NBT website. Log on using your unique NBT reference number or your South African ID Number.

How do I know if I've passed?

There is no pass mark for the NBT. Rather, each institution and programme uses Benchmark Levels.

GENERAL ADVICE

Start Early

It is much easier to prepare if you practice little and often. Start your preparation well in advance; ideally by May. This way you will have plenty of time to complete as many practice questions as you wish to feel comfortable and won't have to panic and cram just before the test, which is a much less effective and more stressful way to learn. In general, an early start will give you the opportunity to identify the complex issues and work at your own pace.

Prioritise

Some questions can be long and complex – and given the intense time pressure you need to know your limits. It is essential that you don't get stuck with very difficult questions. If a question looks particularly long or complex, mark it for review and move on. You don't want to be caught 5 questions short at the end just because you took more time answering a challenging question.

If a question is taking too long, choose a sensible answer and move on. Remember that each question carries equal weighting and therefore, you should adjust your timing accordingly. With practice and discipline, you can get very good at this and learn to maximise your efficiency.

Positive Marking

There are no penalties for incorrect answers in the NBT; you will gain one for each right answer and will not get one for each wrong or unanswered one. This provides you with the luxury that you can always guess should you absolutely be not able to figure out the right answer for a question or run behind time. If you aren't sure (and are running short of time), then make an educated guess and move on. Before 'guessing' you should try to eliminate a couple of answers to increase your chances of getting the question correct.

Avoid losing easy marks on other questions because of poor exam technique. Similarly, if you have failed to finish the exam, take the last 10 seconds to guess the remaining questions to at least give yourself a chance of getting them right.

Practice

This is the best way of familiarising yourself with the style of questions and the timing. You are unlikely to be familiar with the test when first encounter it. Therefore, you want to be comfortable before you sit the real thing.

Practising questions will put you at ease and make you more comfortable with the exam. The more comfortable you are, the less you will panic on the test day and the more likely you are to score highly. Initially, work through the questions at your own pace, and spend time carefully reading the questions and looking at any additional data. When it becomes closer to the test, **make sure you practice the questions under exam conditions**.

Past Papers

The NBT is a very new exam so there aren't sample papers available, and at present, past paper aren't being released either.. Specimens are freely available online at https://nbt.ac.za. Once you've worked your way through the questions in this book, you are highly advised to attempt them.

Repeat Questions

When checking through answers, pay particular attention to questions you have got wrong. Study the worked solution carefully until you feel confident that you understand the reasoning, and then repeat the question without help to check that you can do it. This is the best way to learn from your mistakes, and means you are less likely to make similar mistakes when it comes to the test. The same applies for questions which you were unsure of and made an educated guess which was correct (even if you got it right). When working through this book, **make sure you highlight any questions you are unsure of**, this means you know to spend more time looking over them once marked.

Calculators

You aren't permitted to use calculators in the NBT– thus, it is essential that you have strong numerical skills. For instance, you should be able to rapidly convert between percentages, decimals and fractions. You will seldom get questions that would require calculators but you would be expected to be able to arrive at a sensible estimate. Consider for example:

Estimate 3.962 x 2.322:

3.962 is approximately 4 and 2.323 is approximately 2.33 $= \frac{7}{3}$.

Thus, $3.962 \times 2.322 \approx 4 \times \frac{7}{3} = \frac{28}{3} = 9.33$

Since you will rarely be asked to perform difficult calculations, you can use this as a signpost of if you are tackling a question correctly. For example, if you end up having to divide 8,079 by 357 this should raise alarm bells as calculations are rarely this difficult.

Top tip! Don't leave things too late – do small bits early and often rather than a mad cram in the week before your test. Some of the principles tested in NBT require a great degree of understanding and you don't do yourself justice by trying to cram them into a few hours!

A word on timing...
"If you had all day to do your NBT, you would get 100%. But you don't."

Whilst this isn't completely true, it illustrates a very important point. Once you've practiced and know how to answer the questions, the clock is your biggest enemy. This seemingly obvious statement has one very important consequence. **The way to improve your NBT score is to improve your speed.** There is no magic bullet. But there are a great number of techniques that, with practice, will give you significant time gains, allowing you to answer more questions and score more marks.

Timing is tight throughout the NBT – **mastering timing is the first key to success**. Some candidates choose to work as quickly as possible to save up time at the end to check back, but this is generally not the best way to do it. NBT questions can have a lot of information in them – each time you start answering a question it takes time to get familiar with the instructions and information. By splitting the question into two sessions (the first run-through and the return-to-check) you double the amount of time you spend on familiarising yourself with the data, as you must do it twice instead of only once. This costs valuable time. In addition, candidates who do check back may spend 2–3 minutes doing so and yet not make any actual changes. Whilst this can be reassuring, it is a false reassurance as it is unlikely to have a significant effect on your actual score. Therefore, it is usually best to pace yourself very steadily, aiming to spend the same amount of time on each question and finish the final question in a section just as time runs out. This reduces the time spent on re-familiarising with questions and maximises the time spent on the first attempt, gaining more marks.

It is essential that you don't get stuck with the hardest questions – no doubt there will be some. In the time spent answering only one of these you may miss out on answering three easier questions. If a question is taking too long, choose a sensible answer and move on. Never see this as giving up or in any way failing, rather it is the smart way to approach a test with a tight time limit. With practice and discipline, you can get very good at this and learn to maximise your efficiency. It is not about being a hero and aiming for full marks – this is almost impossible and very much unnecessary. It is about maximising your efficiency and gaining the maximum possible number of marks within the time you have.

Top tip! Ensure that you take a watch that can show you the time in seconds into the exam. This will allow you to have a much more accurate idea of the time you're spending on a question.

ACADEMIC LITERACY (AL)

THE BASICS

Part I of the NBT is the academic literacy (AL) subtest. It tests your ability to quickly read a passage, find information that is relevant and then analyse statements related to the passage. The idea is to test both your language ability and your ability to make decisions.

You are presented with a passage, upon which you answer questions. You are given a stem and must select the most appropriate response based on the question. There is only one right answer – if more than one answer seems appropriate, the task is to choose the *best* response. Remember that there is no negative marking in the NBT. There will be questions where you aren't certain. If that is the case, then choose an option that seems sensible to you and move on. A clear thought process is key to doing well in the Academic literacy section of the NBT – you will have the opportunity to build that up through the worked examples and practice questions until you're answering like a pro!

This is the first section of the NBT, so you're bound to have some nerves. Ensure that you have been to the toilet because once the exam starts you can't pause and go. Take a few deep breaths and calm yourself down. Try to shut out distractions and get yourself into your exam mindset. If you're well prepared, you can remind yourself of that to help keep calm. See it as a job to do and look at the test as an opportunity.

How to Approach This Section
Time pressure is a recurring theme throughout the NBT, but it is especially important in the Academic Literacy section, where you have a lot of information to take in.

> ***Top tip!*** Though it might initially sound counter-intuitive, it is often best to read the question ***before*** reading the passage. When read the passage knowing what you're looking for, you're likely to find the information you need much more quickly.

You should look carefully to see what the question is asking. Sometimes the question will simply need you to find a phrase in the text. In other instances, your critical thinking skills will be needed and you'll have to carefully analyse the information presented to you.

Extreme Words

Words like "extremely", "always" and "never" can give you useful clues for your answer. Statements which make particularly bold claims are less likely to be true, but remember you need a direct contradiction to be able to conclude that they are false.

To answer an "always" question, you're looking for a definition. Always be a bit suspicious of "never" – make sure you're certain before saying true, as most things are possible.

Prioritise

With NBT, you can leave and come back to any question. **By flagging for review**, you make this easier. Since time is tight, you don't want to waste time on long passages when you could be scoring easier marks. Score the easy marks first, then come back to the harder ones if time allows. If time runs too short, at least take enough time to guess the answers as there's a good chance you could pick up some marks anyway.

Be a Lawyer

Put on your most critical and analytical hat! Carefully analyse the statements like you're in a court room. Then look for the evidence! **Examine the passage closely, looking for evidence** that either supports or contradicts the statement. Remember **you're making decisions based on ONLY the passage**, not using any prior knowledge.

Read the Question First

Follow our top tip and read the question before the passage. There is simply not enough time to read all the passages thoroughly and still have time to complete everything. By reading the statement or question first, you can understand what it is that is required of you and can then pick out the appropriate area in the passage. Do not fall into the trap of trying to read all the passage, you will not score highly enough if you do this.

When skim reading through the passage, it is inevitable that you will lose accuracy. However, you can reduce this effect by doing plenty of practice so your ability to glean what you need improves. A good tip is to practice reading short sections of complicated texts, such as quality newspapers or novels, at high pace. Then test yourself to see how much you can recall from the passage.

Find the Keywords

The keyword is the most important word to help you relate the question to the passage; sometimes there might be two keywords in a question. When you read the passage, focus in on the keywords straight away. This gives you something to look for in the passage to identify the right place to work from.

It is usually easy to find the keyword/s, and you'll become even better with practice. When you find it, go back a line and read from the line before through the keyword to the end of the line after. Usually, this contains enough relevant information to give you the answer.

If this is not successful, you need to consider your next steps. Time is very tight in the NBT and especially so in the AL section of the test. There are other passages that need your attention, and there may be much easier marks waiting for you. If reading around the keyword has not given you the right answer it may well be time to move on. It might be that there is a more subtle reference somewhere else, that you need to read the whole passage to reach the answer or indeed that the answer cannot be deduced from the passage. Either way, if it's difficult to find your time could be better spent gaining marks elsewhere. Make a sensible guess and move on.

Use only the Passage

Your answer *must* only be based on the information available in the passage. Do not try and guess the answer based on your general knowledge as this can be a trap. For example, if the question asks who the first person was to walk on the moon, then states "the three crew members of the first lunar mission were Edwin Aldrin, Neil Armstrong and Michael Collins". The correct answer is "cannot tell" – even though you know it was Neil Armstrong and see his name, the passage itself does not tell you who left the landing craft first. Likewise, if there is a quotation or an extract from a book which is factually inaccurate, you should answer based on the information available to you rather than what you know to be true.

If you have not been able to select the correct answer, eliminate as many of the statements as possible and guess.

Flagging for Review

There is an additional option to flag a question for review. **Flagging for review has absolutely no effect on the overall score.** All it does is mark the question in an easy way for it to be revisited if you have time later in the section. Once the section is complete, you cannot return to any questions, flagged or unflagged.

Coming back to questions can be inefficient – you have to read the instructions and data each time you work on the question to know what to do, so by coming back again you double the amount of time spent on doing this, leaving less time for actually answering questions. We feel the best strategy is to work steadily through the questions at a consistent and even pace.

That said, flagging for review has one great utility in the AL section of NBT. If you come across a particularly long or technical passage, you may want to flag for review immediately and skip on to the next passage. By coming back to the passage at the end, you allow yourself the remaining time on the hardest question. This has an advantage in each of two scenarios. If you're really tight for time, at least you maximised the time you did have answering the easier questions, thereby maximising your marks. If it turns out you have extra time to spare, you can spend it on the hardest question, allowing you a better chance to get marks you otherwise would have struggled to obtain. Thus, flagging for review can be useful, but its usefulness is probably greatest when you flag questions very soon after seeing them rather than when you have already spent time trying to find the answer.

Remember to find the right balance: if you flag too many questions you will be overloaded and won't have time to focus on them all; if you flag too few, you risk under-utilising this valuable resource. You should flag only a few questions per section to allow you to properly focus on them if you have spare

EXAMPLE

Before the 20th century, relatively little was known about the atom. The concept that objects were made of smaller particles that could not become any smaller was theorised by two Greek philosophers; Leucippus and Democritus. They believed that if you keep cutting an object consistently, there will come a point where it will not be able to be cut any further. Therefore, the theory of the atom was established but it was not possible to explore it further.

In 1897, JJ Thompson discovered the electron. He subjected a hot metal coil into an electric field, thereby producing the first cathode ray. Importantly, he noticed that the cathode ray could be deflected by a magnetic field, when viewed under a cloud chamber, and realised that it was negatively charged. As the atom is neutral, he proposed that there must be positively charged particles that give the atom an overall neutrality. JJ Thompson put forward the plum pudding model theory of the atom; that positively charged particles and negatively charged particles are mixed together in an infinitely small region of space.

In 1911, Ernest Rutherford carried out the gold leaf experiment. He fired alpha particles at a gold leaf and found that although most of the alpha particles went through, some were deflected. Occasionally, he also saw a small spark upon collision. From this, he theorised that the atom cannot be a mixture of negatively and positively charged particles, but rather has a dense core of positively charged particles. He called these particles protons. He also realised that most of the atom is empty space.

In 1932, James Chadwick performed an experiment that discovered the final component of the atom. On observation of alpha decay, he noticed that one of the particles being emitted was not deflected by a magnetic field, hence being neutrally charged. He called this particle the neutron.

Thus, the Rutherford Model of the Atom was born; the protons and neutrons form the nucleus of the atom, which electrons in spinning in orbit.

> This is a long passage. Consider flagging for review and coming back later if you have time

1. The passage supports which of the following conclusions?
A. The experiments of the previous scientist led to the development and guidance of the other.
B. The Rutherford Atomic Model cannot be further improved.
C. Rutherford had the help of other scientists to put forward his theory.
D. The deflection of the cathode ray by magnetism was the phenomenon that led JJ Thompson to develop the Plum Pudding model.

2. Based on the passage, each of these statements is true except
A. Earnest Rutherford is from New Zealand.
B. James Chadwick named the neutron.
C. The direction of particle deflection was determined using the cloud chamber.
D. Most of the atom is empty space.

3. Using the information in the passage, it can be inferred that:
A. Previous to Leucippus and Democritus, no one had thought of the idea of the atom.
B. Rutherford is the father of nuclear physics.
C. The gold leaf experiment was key in discovering the atomic nucleus.
D. The positron also exists.

4. Which of the following statements about the work of Earnest Rutherford is true?
A. He never carried out his own experiments without assistance from others.
B. The experimental data from the gold leaf experiment led to the development of the Geiger counter.
C. He discovered that most of the atom is empty space.
D. The foundation of nuclear fission was built from the gold leaf experiment.

Answers

1. **D** – D is the only conclusion supported by the passage, none of the other statements are mentioned in the passage. You may know from your general knowledge or simply from common sense that Rutherford had the help of other scientists, but because the passage does not mention this, it is not the answer.

2. **A** – Earnest Rutherford was indeed from New Zealand, but this is not mentioned in the passage.

3. **C** – There is no way that you know that A is true. The passage does not suggest that Rutherford is considered to be the father of nuclear physics. Finally, although the positron does indeed exist, this is not mentioned in the passage!

4. **C** – A and B are also true but not supported in the passage. D is not mentioned in the passage and also not scientifically correct.

ACADEMIC LITERACY QUESTIONS

SET 1
J.S. Mill describes his ethical theory and the reception of this in his book, 'Utilitarianism', and states:

'The creed which accepts as the foundation of morals, Utility, or the Greatest Happiness Principle, holds that actions are right in proportion as they tend to promote happiness, wrong as they tend to produce the reverse of happiness. By happiness is intended pleasure, and the absence of pain; by unhappiness, pain, and the privation of pleasure. To give a clear view of the moral standard set up by the theory, much more requires to be said; in particular, what things it includes in the ideas of pain and pleasure; and to what extent this is left an open question. But these supplementary explanations do not affect the theory of life on which this theory of morality is grounded—namely, that pleasure, and freedom from pain, are the only things desirable as ends; and that all desirable things are desirable either for the pleasure inherent in themselves, or as means to the promotion of pleasure and the prevention of pain.

Now, such a theory of life provokes in many minds, and among them in some of the most estimable in feeling and purpose, dislike. To suppose that life has (as they express it) no higher end than pleasure—no better and nobler object of desire and pursuit—they designate as utterly mean and grovelling; as a doctrine worthy only of swine, to whom the followers of Epicurus were, at a very early period, contemptuously likened; and modern holders of the doctrine are occasionally made the subject of equally polite comparisons by its German, French, and English assailants.

When thus attacked, the Epicureans have always answered, that it is not they, but their accusers, who represent human nature in a degrading light; since the accusation supposes human beings to be capable of no pleasures except those of which swine are capable.'

1. How do the Epicureans answer their critics?
A. By claiming the critics are miserable, in their refusal to embrace pleasure.
B. That the critics do not understand the multiplicity of things contained in the word 'pleasure'.
C. By calling their critics degraded.
D. By suggesting their critics are more susceptible to animalistic pleasures than they.

2. Which of the following actions are NOT in keeping with the theory of utility?
A. Providing a crash mat for a gymnast, to prevent him or her hurting him or herself.
B. Getting a crash mat for yourself, to prevent hurting yourself when performing gymnastics.
C. Not eating a chocolate bar because social pressures deem it wrong.
D. Eating a chocolate bar because it is delicious.

3. Which of the following does the passage suggest about critics of utilitarianism?
A. They are Christians.
B. They are European.
C. They are unintelligent.
D. They are reactionary.

4. Utilitarianism is only concerned with ends.
A. True   B. False   C. Can't tell

5. The above passage defines:
A. What is included by the term pleasure
B. What is included by the term pain
C. What is meant by Epicureanism
D. What is meant by utility

2 / 5

22

SET 2

Geology deals with the rocks of the earth's crust. It learns from their composition and structure how the rocks were made and how they have been modified. It ascertains how they have been brought to their present places and wrought to their various topographic forms, such as hills and valleys, plains and mountains. It studies the vestiges, which the rocks preserve, of ancient organisms that once inhabited our planet. Geology is the history of the earth and its inhabitants, as read in the rocks of the earth's crust.

To obtain a general idea of the nature and method of our science before beginning its study in detail, we may visit some valley, on whose sides are rocky ledges. Here the rocks lie in horizontal layers. Although only their edges are exposed, we may infer that these layers run into the upland on either side and underlie the entire district; they are part of the foundation of solid rock found beneath the loose materials of the surface everywhere.

Take the sandstones ledge of a valley. Looking closely at the rock we see that it is composed of myriads of grains of sand cemented together. These grains have been worn and rounded. They are sorted also, those of each layer being about of a size. By some means they have been brought hither from some more ancient source. Surely these grains have had a history before they here found a resting place—a history which we are to learn to read.

The successive layers of the rock suggest that they were built one after another from the bottom upward. We may be as sure that each layer was formed before those above it as that the bottom courses of stone in a wall were laid before the courses which rest upon them.

6. Based on the passage, each of these statements can be verified, EXCEPT?
A. We can learn about earth's inhabitants through its crust.
B. Individual layers of sandstone form one after another.
C. Rocks are made of sand.
D. Geology does not always demand explicit evidence.

23

7. Wall-building is used in this passage to help us understand:
A. Mountains
B. Valleys
C. Hills
D. Plains

8. The sand mentioned in the passage comes from:
A. An ancient beach
B. The sea
C. The earth's crust
D. It is undisclosed

9. A foundation of rock is **NOT** found underneath:
A. Upland
B. Lowland
C. Nowhere
D. Water

10. 'Grains of sand' are described as sorted by:
A. Shape
B. Texture
C. Age
D. Measurements

SET 3

The genus of plants called Narcissus, many of the species of which are highly esteemed by the floriculturist and lover of cultivated plants, belongs to the Amaryllis family (Amaryllidaceæ.) This family includes about seventy genera and over eight hundred species that are mostly native in tropical or semi-tropical countries, though a few are found in temperate climates.

Many of the species are sought for ornamental purposes and, on account of their beauty and remarkable odour, they are more prized by many than are the species of the Lily family. In this group is classed the American Aloe (Agave Americana) valued not only for cultivation, but also by the Mexicans on account of the sweet fluid which is yielded by its central bud. This liquid, after fermentation, forms an intoxicating liquor known as pulque. By distillation, this yields a liquid, very similar to rum, called by the Mexicans mescal. The leaves furnish a strong fibre, known as vegetable silk, from which, since remote times, paper has been manufactured.

The popular opinion is that this plant flowers but once in a century; hence the name 'Century Plant' is often applied to it, though under proper culture it will blossom more frequently.

11. Which of the following are **NOT** mentioned as potential uses for a narcissus plant:
A. Perfume production
B. Alcohol production
C. Visual decoration
D. Stationary production

12. Why is the plant known as 'the century plant'?
A. It is sown only once every hundred years.
B. It can only able to be fertilised once a century.
C. It is perceived as blooming centennially.
D. It can only able to flower once within a hundred years.

13. Which of the following statements is most supported by the above passage:
A. Lilies are generally valued less than members of the Narcissus genus.
B. Lilies are famously not as attractive as members of the Narcissus genus.
C. A number are people prefer members of the Narcissus genus over Lilies.
D. Members of the Narcissus genus are a welcome addition to any household.

14. Which of the following statements is NOT true:
A. American Aloe can be used to make rum.
B. The Amaryllis family contains more than six hundred species of Narcissus.
C. Members of the Narcissus genus can be found in all climates.
D. The members of the Narcissus genus have a distinctive smell.

15. Which of the following statements can be verified by the passage:
A. The 'Narcissus' genus is named after the mythical character, famed for his beauty.
B. Agave syrup can be collected by American Aloe.
C. A genus belongs to a family.
D. Members of the Narcissus genus are used for their soothing properties.

25

SET 4

The following passage is found in a book on nature published in 1899:

Five women out of every ten who walk the streets of Chicago and other Illinois cities, says a prominent journal, by wearing dead birds upon their hats proclaim themselves as lawbreakers. For the first time in the history of Illinois laws it has been made an offense punishable by fine and imprisonment, or both, to have in possession any dead, harmless bird except game birds, which may be possessed in their proper season. The wearing of a tern, or a gull, a woodpecker, or a jay is an offense against the law's majesty, and any policeman with a mind rigidly bent upon enforcing the law could round up, without a written warrant, a wagon load of the offenders any hour in the day, and carry them off to the lockup. What moral suasion cannot do, a crusade of this sort undoubtedly would.

Thanks to the personal influence of the Princess of Wales, the osprey plume, so long a feature of the uniforms of a number of the cavalry regiments of the British army, has been abolished. After Dec. 31, 1899, the osprey plume, by order of Field Marshal Lord Wolseley, is to be replaced by one of ostrich feathers. It was the wearing of these plumes by the officers of all the hussar and rifle regiments, as well as of the Royal Horse Artillery, which so sadly interfered with the crusade inaugurated by the Princess against the use of osprey plumes. The fact that these plumes, to be of any marketable value, have to be torn from the living bird during the nesting season induced the Queen, the Princess of Wales, and other ladies of the royal family to set their faces against the use of both the osprey plume and the aigrette as articles of fashionable wear.

16. In 1899:
A. Women across the USA could be prosecuted for owning ornamental dead birds.
B. There was a significant rise of female arrests in America.
C. Possession of a dead gull could lead to trouble.
D. Americans responded to law by citing the use of jays as ornamentation unfashionable.

17. Ostrich feathers were seen as preferable to osprey plums because:
A. Ostriches are less intelligent birds.
B. Ostriches are killed for their meat, so one might as well use their feathers.
C. Queen Elizabeth has an especial love of ospreys.
D. Harvesting osprey feathers was seen as an inhumane process.

18. Games birds could be possessed by citizens of Illinois all year round.
A. True   B. False   C. Can't tell

19. Banning Osprey feathers in the UK's army was difficult because:
A. Many uniforms required them.
B. The Princess did not have the authority to implement the ban.
C. Her ultimate support was predominately female, and thus their concerns seemed to have no relevance from the male domain of the army.
D. It would be hard to differentiate between other regiments within the army, who were already wearing ostrich feathers.

20. Which of the following could NOT be legally owned in Illinois, according to the passage:
A. A live bird intended for personal ornamentation.
B. A dead bird of prey that had violently attacked you.
C. Feathered garments.
D. None of the above.

5/5

SET 5

Indie game developer Lucas Pope created 'Papers Please', a video game where the player is an immigration officer processing people attempting to enter Arstotzka, a fictional dystopia. Released in 2013, the game was originally made for Microsoft Windows and OS X platforms. It was subsequently released for Linux and the iPad in 2014.

27

The game is set in 1982, and gameplay involves the player processing large numbers of applicants attempting to enter the country, through checking various pieces of paperwork. This is intended to keep criminals out, whether they are terrorists or drug smugglers. When looking through the applicant's 'papers', discrepancies may be discovered: the player must then enquire about these and may go on to use other tools, such as a body scanner and finger printing to discover the truth of the candidate's motives. Applicants may attempt to bribe the officer in order to get through. Ultimately, the game player must stamp candidates passports, either accepting into or rejecting them from the country. Their work is being monitored, however: after two false acceptances/rejections, the player will be pecuniarily punished, with their day's wages being decreased in response to their administrative sloppiness. They have a limited amount of time, representing each 'day', to work, during which they will be paid in accordance to the number of people processed.

21. Which of the following statements is best supported by the above passage:
A. Lucas Pope created the Papers Please for a small games company.
B. Papers Please is a multi-platform game.
C. Arstotzka is a fictionalised version of an ex-Soviet block state.
D. The game gained significant media attention in 2014.

22. Which of the following statements best sums up the official job of the player's character:
A. To accept as many applicants into Artstotzka as possible.
B. To reject as many new applicants entering Arstotzka as possible.
C. To avoid making mistakes in processing people.
D. To stamp passports.

23. Discrepancies in information provided by applicants lead to the player:
A. Interrogating and performing a fingerprint check on the suspicious individual.
B. Interrogating and performing a full body scan on the suspicious individual.
C. Asking the suspicious individual for further information.
D. Performing one or multiple physical assessments of the individual.

24. Which of the following statements is true:
A. The game-player solely makes money through processing applicants.
B. The game-player will ultimately be responsible for multiple arrests.
C. The game-player will not be forgiven for their mistakes.
D. The game-player may be subject to fiscal penalisation.

SET 6

Emerging in 1970s USA, Blaxploitation, or 'blacksploitation', gives homage to many other genres: within it, there are western, martial arts films, musicals, coming-of-age dramas and comedies, and the genre has even parodied itself with films like 'Black Dynamite'. Blaxploitation movies may take place in the South, and focus on issues like slavery, or be set in the poor neighbourhoods of the Northeast or West coast, but in any case they will feature a predominately black cast. It is also known to feature soundtracks comprised of soul and funk music, and the common feature of character's using the words 'honky', 'cracker' and other slurs against white people.

Originally, the genre's exports were aimed at city-dwelling black Americans, but their appeal has since grown and is not exclusive to any race. Despite the negative sound of the title 'blaxploitation', the term was coined by ex-film publicist Junius Griffin, the then head of LA's NAACP, National Association for the Advancement of Coloured People. He came up with the name through a play on the word 'sexploitation' describing films which featured pornographic scenes.

The film 'Shaft' and 'Sweet Sweetback's Baadasssss Song' are two of the forerunners of this genre, both released in 1971. The latter has been said, by Variety, to have created the genre

25. Which of the following statements is supported by the information in the above passage:
A. 'Blaxploitation' was a term coined by porn directors moving into a new genre.
B. 'Blaxploitation' was a term made popular by black audiences.
C. 'Blaxploitation' was a term coined by a civil rights activist.
D. 'Blaxploitation' was a term criticised by white sympathisers.

29

26. Which of the following statements best describes the most common element of a Blaxploitation film:
A. Characters performing funk songs.
B. Characters coming to terms with the legacy of slavery.
C. Characters performing martial arts.
D. Characters using racial slurs.

27. Which of these statements best describes casting in Blaxploitation films:
A. Primarily white   C. Exclusively white
B. Primarily black   D. Exclusively black

28. Which of the following best describes the audiences of Blaxploitation films:
A. Originally for all middle-class African-Americans.
B. Originally for all urban-dwellers.
C. Multi-ethnic.
D. Shrinking since the mid-1970s.

29. The legacy of films including soft-core porn is knowingly acknowledged in the name of two Blaxploitation titles, 'Shaft' and 'Sweet Sweetback's Baadasssss song', both of which suggest body parts associated with sex films.
A. True   B. False   C. Can't tell

30

SET 7

When discussing his famous character Rorschach, the antihero of 'Watchmen', Moore explains, 'I originally intended Rorschach to be a warning about the possible outcome of vigilante thinking. But an awful lot of comic readers felt his remorseless, frightening, psychotic toughness was his most appealing characteristic – not quite what I was going for.' Moore misunderstands his own hero's appeal within this quotation: it is not that Rorschach is willing to break little fingers to extract information, or that he is happy to use violence, that makes him laudable. The Comedian, another 'superhero' within the alternative world of Watchmen, is a thug who has won no great fan base; his remorselessness (killing a pregnant Vietnamese woman), frightening (attempt at rape), psychotic toughness (one only has to look at the panels of him shooting out into a crowd to witness this) is repulsive, not winning. This is because The Comedian has no purpose: he is a nihilist, and as a nihilist, denies any potential meaning to his fellow man, and so to the comic's reader. Everything to him is a 'joke', including his self, and consequently his own death could be seen as just another gag.

Rorschach, on the other hand, does believe in something: he questions if his fight for justice 'is futile?' then instantly corrects himself, stating 'there is good and evil, and evil must be punished. Even in the face of Armageddon I shall not compromise in this.' Jacob Held, in his essay comparing Rorschach's motivation with Kantian ethics, put forward the postulation 'perhaps our dignity is found in acting as if the world were just, even when it is clearly not.' Rorschach then causes pain in others not because he is a sadist, but because he feels the need to punish wrong and to uphold the good, and though he cannot make the world just, he can act according to his sense of justice - through the use of violence.

30. Which of the following best describes 'Watchmen':
A. A book that contains only vicious characters.
B. An expression of despair when contemplating an imperfect world.
C. An example of how an author's intentions are not always realised.
D. A book that accidentally glamorises violence.

31. 'The Comedian' is a misnomer - the character that goes by this title should not, logically, be called this.
A. True   B. False   C. Can't tell

32. Which of the following best articulates the view put forward by Jacob Held?
A. We find dignity through just actions.
B. If one decides to behave as though the world is fair, this may lead to a discovery of self-worth.
C. It is shameful to view the world as corrupt.
D. Self-value can only be found in madness.

33. What does the passage above argue?
A. Rorschach breaking little fingers is preferable to the Comedian attempting rape somebody.
B. The Comedian's depressing sense of humour has made him unpopular.
C. Rorschach is not actually violent.
D. Rorschach is popular because his aggressive behaviour has a moral intent, and is not just violence.

34. What does the word 'nihilist' mean in the context of the passage?
A. Someone who believes there is no meaning to life.
B. Someone who is full of anger at the corruption of society.
C. Someone who is narcissistic.
D. Someone who hates other people.

SET 8

'The Bechdel Test', also known as the 'Mo Movie Measure' and 'The Bechdel Rule' is named after cartoonist Alison Bechdel, who in 1985 wrote a cartoon containing the original proposal of the 'test'. It depicts one woman telling another that she has 'a rule' that she will only see a film if it satisfies three basic requirements: that it contains at least two women, that they talk to each other and that their conversation is on something other than a man. The second woman states that this is 'pretty strict, but a good idea', to which the first responds the last film she saw that complied with this was 'Alien'. The original notion described in the strip has been attributed to Liz Wallace, and the test is sometimes referred to as the Bechdel/Wallace Test.

Following this, a website entitled 'The Bechdel Test Movie List' has formed an extensive list of cinematic output, showing movies that pass and do not pass the test. One may be surprised at the number of movies that would not be watched by first woman in the Bechdel comic: many blockbusters do not make the mark, and such titles as 'Godzilla', 'The Imitation Game' and 'Robocop' all feature on the list of 'failed' films.

35. According to The Bechdel Test, 'The Imitation Game' is a sexist film.
A. True   B. False   C. Can't tell

36. Which of the following films would pass the Bechdel test:
A. One where the only conversation between two women is on woman A's brother.
B. One where there are two conversations, one on woman A's son and another on woman B's boss, Mr Smith.
C. One where there are five women, in which at one point they all have a chat about how to lose weight and the best hair removal techniques.
D. One where there is one woman who chats about all manner of things with her male colleagues, including her USA presidential campaign.

37. 50% of horror films, according to the above extract, pass the Bechdel test.
A. True   B. False   C. Can't tell

38. Which of the following phrases best describes the reaction of the second woman within the comic strip:
A. Ecstatically approving   C. Cautiously approving
B. Condemning   D. Apathetic

39. The two women in the comic strip are manifestations of Bechdel and Wallace, with the piece of art being a recreation of their original conversation on this matter.
A. True   B. False   C. Can't tell

SET 9

There are many comic tropes a comedian or group of comedians may want to employ in their set or act, but for the purpose of this extract we shall focus on the device of the 'call-back'. A call-back is a reference made to a previous joke, in a different context: for example, a comedian may make the joke 'why did the chicken cross the road? To get to the other side' early on in his or her set, and then later on may reference this again by telling an anecdote and saying 'so then I crossed the road - oh, look, there's a chicken! Strange, I could have sworn he was over there a moment ago'. Though the call-back may appear to simply rely on the idea that repetition is inherently funny, it actually has several desirable effects. Firstly, it means that one joke can provide more than one laugh, as the memory of the previous joke encourages renewed chuckling, and so the original quip's comic potential is increased. It also builds up a relationship between comedian and audience, as it builds up a sense of familiarity with the speaker and his or her subject matter, and this bond also may encourage more laughter - the second joke creates the same feeling as an 'in-joke'. If used at the end of a set - as a call-back often is - it gives a sense of completion, and also may lead to the ending of the act culminating in the largest laugh.

In TV, a call-back often refers to a joke made in a previous episode.

40. Repetition is inherently funny.
A. True   B. False   C. Can't tell

41. Which of the following best explains how a call-back works:
A. Previous understanding of a subject makes it potentially more comic.
B. Doubling a joke makes it potentially twice as funny.
C. Making the audience feel comfortable is more likely to make them laugh.
D. We find people we have a relationship with funny.

42. For a call-back to work, the original joke has to be significantly funny.
A. True   B. False   C. Can't tell

43. A call-back cannot be used in an un-comic setting.
A. True   B. False   C. Can't tell

34

44. Which of the following statements is best supported by the above passage:
A. A call-back is used to create a sense of the circle having fully come to pass.
B. A call-back can be a useful addition to an individual comedian's set.
C. A call-back creates unity through disparate TV episodes.
D. A call-back is an especially important trope to consider.

SET 10

Harriet Beecher (Stowe) was born June 14, 1811, in the characteristic New England town of Litchfield, Connecticut. Her father was the Rev. Dr. Lyman Beecher, a distinguished Calvinistic divine, her mother Roxanna Foote, his first wife. Harriet Beecher was ushered into a household of happy, healthy children, and found five brothers and sisters awaiting her. The eldest was Catherine, born September 6, 1800. Following her were two sturdy boys, William and Edward; then came Mary, then George, and at last Harriet. Another little Harriet was actually born three years before, but died when aged only one month old; the fourth daughter, the subject of this passage, was named in memory of this sister Harriet Elizabeth. Just two years after Harriet was born, in the same month, another brother, Henry Ward, was welcomed to the family circle, and after him came Charles, the last of Roxanna Beecher's children.

The first memorable incident of Harriet's life was the death of her mother, which occurred when she was four years old, and which ever afterwards remained with her as the most tender, sad and sacred memory of her childhood. Mrs Stowe's recollections of her mother are found in a letter to her brother Charles, afterwards published in the 'Autobiography and Correspondence of Lyman Beecher.' She says: —

"I was between three and four years of age when our mother died, and my personal recollections of her are therefore but few. But the deep interest and veneration that she inspired in all who knew her were such that during all my childhood I was constantly hearing her spoken of, and from one friend or another some incident or anecdote of her life was constantly being impressed upon me.

45. Harriet, the main character in the article, was the third daughter of Roxanna Beecher:

A. True   B. False   C. Can't tell

46. Which of the following statements, according to the passage, are true:
A. Harriet Beecher had a religious father.
B. Harriet Beecher was born in the English town Litchfield.
C. Harriet Beecher was born in the 18th century.
D. Harriet Beecher was born in an average American town.

47. Roxanna Beecher was an admired woman.
A. True   B. False   C. Can't tell

48. Harriet Beecher Stowe's mother's death is described as:
A. Her saddest memory of her life.
B. The earliest significant event in her life.
C. Her most tender memory of her life.
D. All of the above.

49. Which of the following statements is supported by the above passage:
A. Harriet Beecher was between three and four when her mother died.
B. Harriet Beecher had five brothers waiting for her when she was born.
C. Harriet Beecher was a letter-writer.
D. Harriet Beecher was an autobiographer.

SET 11

Gutenberg's father was a man of good family. Very likely the boy was taught to read. But the books from which he learned were not like ours; they were written by hand. A better name for them than books is 'manuscripts,' which means handwritings.

While Gutenberg was growing up a new way of making books came into use, which was a great deal better than copying by hand. It was what is called block printing. The printer first cut a block of hard wood the size of the page that he was going to print. Then he cut out every word of the written page upon the smooth face of his block. This had to be very carefully done. When it was finished the printer had to cut away the wood from the sides of every letter. This left the letters raised, as the letters are in books now printed for the blind.

The block was now ready to be used. The letters were inked, paper was laid upon them and pressed down. With blocks the printer could make copies of a book a great deal faster than a man could write them by hand. But the making of the blocks took a long time, and each block would print only one page.

Gutenberg enjoyed reading the manuscripts and block books that his parents and their wealthy friends had; and he often said it was a pity that only rich people could own books. Finally he determined to contrive some easy and quick way of printing.

50. Which of the following reasons can be inferred from the above passage to explain Gutenberg's desire to create a new way of printing was:
A. It was a lucrative business to go into.
B. He wanted to make text more accessible.
C. He was tired of waiting for each book to be hand written or block pressed, and wanted quicker access to literature.
D. He found the current books too costly for him to continue his reading habit.

51. Which of the following is **NOT** mentioned as a concern of block printing?
A. It exhausts the carver.
B. It is intricate and demands attention to detail.
C. It is a lengthy process.
D. An individual block has limited utility.

52. Which of the following statements is definitely true according to the above passage?
A. Gutenberg was taught to read as a boy.
B. Gutenberg's father belonged to the aristocracy.
C. Block printing was the predominant book manufacturing process whilst Gutenberg was growing up.
D. Gutenberg's family was somewhat sociable.

53. Printing with the block process was a simple task of inking up the prepared block and pressing it down on a piece of paper, to make one page of the text.
A. True B. False C. Can't tell

54. Which of the following statements are **NOT** supported by the above passage:
A. Manuscripts were beautifully crafted.
B. 'Manuscripts' is an appropriate name for what it describes.
C. Block printing is an appropriate name for what it describes.
D. Having well off friends was a good way to expand your reading.

SET 12

Cassandra may be considered an odd name to give your daughter, when you consider the mythical significance of it. Cassandra was a figure in ancient Greek mythology, a Trojan girl born to King Priam, who had been cursed: she had the gift of prophecy, but no one would believe in her words. She ultimately ends up taken from her homeland, as the sexual slave of Agamemnon. Agamemnon's wife then slaughters the girl, and one might wonder why any parent would name their daughter after such an ill-fated figure.

There are several stories that explain how Cassandra gained her gift and her curse. One narrative states that the god Apollo gave the girl the ability to tell the future, in an attempt to seduce her. When she refused him, he corrupted her gift. Another version tells us that Cassandra originally told Apollo she would have sex with him, in exchange for the gift of prophecy. When she subsequently refused him, having attained this power, he then spat in her mouth during a kiss, and this action made her ever after doomed to be disbelieved.

The figure of Cassandra has been presented in various pieces of classical literature, including Homer's epic poem 'The Iliad', Euripides' 'Trojan Women' and Aeschylus' 'The Agamemnon'. Although the presentation of her character alters in the different manifestation, the tragic fate of the woman is known within the different texts, as it would be known by the different authors and audiences of these works.

55. Throughout mythology, Apollo is always presented as the figure who gives Cassandra prophecy.
A. True   B.   False   C.   Can't tell

56. Which of the following statements is best supported by the passage:
A. Parents who call their daughter Cassandra must hate their children.
B. Cassandra prizes chastity higher than her personal comfort.
C. Cassandra had supernatural powers.
D. Cassandra is often seen as a home wrecker.

57. Which of the following statements is **NOT** supported by the passage:
A. Cassandra comes from a royal line.
B. Cassandra had a happy childhood before her horrible fate.
C. Cassandra has been written about for the stage.
D. Homer has been inspired by Cassandra.

58. Cassandra's personality is consistently presented in the different pieces of literature she is included in.
A. True   B.   False   C.   Can't tell

59. Which of the following is offered in the above passage to explain Apollo's ire:
A. Cassandra breaking her promise.
B. Cassandra not accepting his gift.
C. Cassandra demanding more gifts.
D. Cassandra not acknowledging his gifts.

SET 13

Despite the fact that some associate musicals with cheesy joy, the genre is not limited to gleeful stories, as can be demonstrated by the macabre musical, 'Sweeney Todd'. The original story of the murderous barber appears in a Victorian penny dreadful, 'The String of Pearls: A Romance'. The penny dreadful material was adapted for the 19th century stage, and in the 20th century was adapted into two separate melodramas, before the story was taken up by Stephen Sondheim and Hugh Wheeler. The pair turned it into a new musical, which has since been performed across the globe and been adapted into a film starring Johnny Depp.

Sondheim and Wheeler's drama tells a disturbing narrative: the protagonist, falsely accused of a crime by a crooked judge, escapes from Australia to be told that his wife was raped by that same man of the court. In response, she has committed suicide, and her daughter - Todd's daughter - has been made the ward of the judge. The eponymous figure ultimately goes on a killing spree, vowing vengeance for the people who have wronged him but also declaring 'we all deserve to die', and acting on this belief by killing many of his clients, men who come to his barbershop. His new partner in crime, Mrs Lovett, comes up with the idea of turning the bodies of his victims into the filling of pies, as a way of sourcing affordable meat - after all, she claims, 'times is hard'.

Cannibalism, vengeance, murder and corruption - these are all themes that demonstrate that this show does not conform to a happy-clappy preconception of its genre.

60. Which of the following statements are best supported by the above passage:
A. Sondheim is a brilliant musician and lyricist.
B. Most musicals deal with morbid themes.
C. Wheeler is an avid penny dreadful fan.
D. Generalisations can be misleading.

61. All the adjectives below are explicitly supported by the passage as ways of describing the crimes described within it, except:

A. Comic
B. Culinary
C. Vengeful
D. Sexual

62. Mrs Lovett and Sweeney Todd are in a romantic relationship.

A. True
B. False
C. Can't tell

63. The best way to describe the belief of Todd as mentioned in the above passage:

A. Bad people should die so good can live and prosper.
B. Good people should die because the bad have basically taken over.
C. All men should die.
D. All humans merit death.

64. Which of the following statements is best supported in the above passage:

A. There are four themes in 'Sweeney Todd'.
B. Legal corruption is the predominate theme of 'Sweeney Todd'.
C. Several 'Sweeney Todd' themes are morbid.
D. There is nothing positive in 'Sweeney Todd'.

SET 14

The United States released the following as part of a pamphlet titled 'If Your Baby Must Travel in Wartime', released during the Second World War:

'Have you been on a train lately? The railroads have a hard job to do these days, but one that they are doing well. But before you decide on a trip with a baby, you should realise what a wartime train is like. So let's look into one.

This train is crowded. At every stop more people get on—more and still more. Soldiers and sailors on furloughs, men on business trips, women — young and not so young — and babies, lots of them, mostly small.

The seats are full. People stand and jostle one another in the aisle. Mothers sit crowded into single seats with toddlers or with babies in their laps. Three sailors occupy space meant for two. A soldier sits on his tipped-up suitcase. A marine leans against the back of the seat. Some people stand in line for 2 hours waiting to get into the diner, some munch sandwiches obtained from the porter or taken out of a paper bag, and some go hungry. And those who get to the diner have had to push their way through five or six moving cars.

You will want to think twice before taking your baby into such a crowded, uncomfortable place as a train. And having thought twice, you'd better decide to stay home unless your trip is absolutely necessary.

But suppose you and your baby must travel. Well then, you will have to plan for the dozens of small but essential things incidental to travelling with a baby and equip yourself to handle them.'

65. First World War passenger trains were exceptionally crowded.
A.   True   B.   False   C.   Can't tell

66. Which of the following phrases is described by the above passage:
A.   A soldier responds to the situation by creating his own seat.
B.   A sailor rest against a seat's back.
C.   Many people queue for over an hour to get to the diner car.
D.   Many go without eating for the duration of a train journey.

67. The pamphlet wishes to increase the number of passengers on trains.
A.   True   B.   False   C.   Can't tell

68. Every station the described train passes through has passengers wanting to get onto the vehicle.
A.   True   B.   False   C.   Can't tell

69. Which of the following does the above passage do:
A.   Compliment the railroads.
B.   Insult passengers who are mothers.
C.   Insult passengers who work for the navy.
D.   Compliment soldiers.

42

SET 15

The following extract is from 'Foods That Will Win the War', published in the USA during the First World War:

'A slice of bread seems an unimportant thing. Yet one good-sized slice of bread weighs an ounce. It contains almost three-fourths of an ounce of flour. If every one of the country's 20,000,000 homes wastes on the average only one such slice of bread a day, the country is throwing away daily over 14,000,000 ounces of flour—over 875,000 pounds, or enough flour for over a million one-pound loaves a day. For a full year at this rate there would be a waste of over 319,000,000 pounds of flour—1,500,000 barrels—enough flour to make 365,000,000 loaves.

As it takes four and one-half bushels of wheat to make a barrel of ordinary flour, this waste would represent the flour from over 7,000,000 bushels of wheat. Fourteen and nine-tenths bushels of wheat on the average are raised per acre. It would take the product of some 470,000 acres just to provide a single slice of bread to be wasted daily in every home.

But someone says, 'a full slice of bread is not wasted in every home.' Very well, make it a daily slice for every four or every ten or every thirty homes—make it a weekly or monthly slice in every home—or make the wasted slice thinner. The waste of flour involved is still appalling. These are figures compiled by government experts, and they should give pause to every housekeeper who permits a slice of bread to be wasted in her home.'

70. According to the above passage, a slice of bread:
A. Contains 1/6 lb. of flour
B. Contains a 1/4-ounce of air
C. Is 75% flour
D. Is one fourth salt, butter and yeast

71. The passage denies that 20,000,000 homes at the point of writing wasted at least a slice of bread a day.
A. True　　　　　　B. False　　　　　　C. Can't tell

43

72. If 20,000,000 homes wasted a slice of bread, this waste would be equal to:
A. One million loaves of bread a day.
B. Over 319,000,000 bushels of flour in 365 days.
C. 1.5 million barrels per annum.
D. Over 365,000 loaves a year.

73. According to the above passage, a slice of bread is an unimportant thing.
A. True   B. False   C. Can't tell

74. Which of the following statements are supported by the above passage:
A. The writer has received much criticism for his views.
B. The government should do more to inform the public about waste.
C. The government has taken responsibility for public waste.
D. Responsibility lies with the person who keeps the house.

SET 16

At the election of President and Vice President of the United States, and members of Congress, in November, 1872, Susan B. Anthony, and several other women, offered their votes to the inspectors of election, claiming the right to vote, as among the privileges and immunities secured to them as citizens by the fourteenth amendment to the Constitution of the United States. The inspectors, Jones, Hall, and Marsh, by a majority, decided in favour of receiving the offered votes, against the dissent of Hall, and they were received and deposited in the ballot box. For this act, the women, fourteen in number, were arrested and held to bail, and indictments were found against them, under the 19th Section of the Act of Congress of May 30th, 1870, (16 St. at L. 144.) independently charging them with the offense of knowingly voting without having a lawful right to vote. The three inspectors were also arrested, but only two of them were held to bail, Hall having been discharged by the Commissioner on whose warrant they were arrested. All three, however were jointly indicted under the same statute—for having knowingly and wilfully received the votes of persons not entitled to vote.

Of the women voters, the case of Miss Anthony alone was brought to trial, a nolle prosequi having been entered upon the other indictments. Upon the trial of Miss Anthony before the U.S. Circuit Court for the Northern District of New York, at Canandaigua, in June, 1873, it was proved that before offering her vote she was advised by her counsel that she had a right to vote; and that she entertained no doubt, at the time of voting, that she was entitled to vote.

75. According to the above passage, how many people in total were arrested due to the group of women voting?
A. Fourteen
B. Three
C. Seventeen
D. Sixteen

76. Susan B. Anthony was the only person brought to trial because of the incident.
A. True
B. False
C. Can't tell

77. Which of the following best describes initial opinions of the election officers:
A. United by each member's personal support of the women's votes.
B. Divided in response to the women's actions.
C. Apathetic about the women's actions.
D. United by general disapproval of the women's actions.

78. Which defence for Susan B. Anthony is mentioned above?
A. She did not realise she was not allowed to vote.
B. That all people born in the USA should be able to vote for their president.
C. That gender should not prevent her vote.
D. The election officers accepted her vote, showing the responsibility is not with her.

79. The women were charged jointly under the same indictment.
A. True
B. False
C. Can't tell

SET 17

The following is taken from a book about Norway published in 1909:

'In a country like Norway, with its vast forests and waste moorlands, it is only natural to find a considerable variety of animals and birds. Some of these are peculiar to Scandinavia. Some, though only occasionally found in the British Isles, are not rare in Norway; whilst others (more especially among the birds) are equally common in both countries.

There was a time when the people of England lived in a state of fear and dread of the ravages of wolves and bears, and the Norwegians of the country districts even now have to guard their flocks and herds from these destroyers. Except in the forest tracts of the Far North, however, bears are not numerous, but in some parts, even in the South, they are sufficiently so to be a nuisance, and are ruthlessly hunted down by the farmers. As far as wolves are concerned civilization is, fortunately, driving them farther afield each year, and only in the most out-of-the-way parts are they ever encountered nowadays.

Stories of packs of hungry wolves following in the wake of a sleigh are still told to the children in Norway, but they relate to bygone times—half a century or more ago, and such wild excitements no longer enter into the Norsemen's lives.'

80. Which of the following is best supported by the above passage:
A. The variety of birds and animals to be found in Norway is unique to that country.
B. The variety of birds and animals to be found in Norway is common to all European countries.
C. By having forests, a country is more likely to have a variety of birds and animals.
D. England and Norway have similar geographical features.

81. English people are described as:
A. Having been anxious of certain animals.
B. Sceptical of bears.
C. Living in fear of wolves.
D. Developmentally behind the Norwegians.

82. Bears are described as:
A. Hunting
B. Scavenging
C. Damaging
D. Man-eating

83. Bears are also:
A. Numerous in all forest tracts.
B. Numerous throughout the North.
C. Numerous throughout the South.
D. At risk in parts of Norway.

84. The passage suggests:
A. The movement of wolves to the out-of-reach parts of Norway is beneficial.
B. Wildlife currently threats Norwegian children.
C. Regret at the loss of adventures.
D. Norsemen particularly respect their natural surroundings.

SET 18

The following extract is taken from Freud's book 'Dream Psychology: Psychoanalysis for Beginners'

In what we may term pre-scientific days, people were in no uncertainty about the interpretation of dreams. When they were recalled after awakening they were regarded as either the friendly or hostile manifestation of some higher powers, demoniacal and divine. With the rise of scientific thought the whole of this expressive mythology was transferred to psychology; today there is but a small minority among educated persons who doubt that the dream is the dreamer's own psychical act.

But since the downfall of the mythological hypothesis an interpretation of the dream has been wanting. The conditions of its origin; its relationship to our psychical life when we are awake; its independence of disturbances which, during the state of sleep, seem to compel notice; its many peculiarities repugnant to our waking thought; the incongruence between its images and the feelings they engender; then the dream's evanescence, the way in which, on awakening, our thoughts thrust it aside as something bizarre, and our reminiscences mutilating or rejecting it—all these and many other problems have for many hundred years demanded answers which up till now could never have been satisfactory. Before all there is the question as to the meaning of the dream, a question that is in itself double-sided. There is, firstly, the psychical significance of the dream, its position with regard to the psychical processes, as to a possible biological function; secondly, has the dream a meaning—can sense be made of each single dream as of other mental syntheses?

85. Dreams used to be regarded as having a potentially religious quality.
A.   True   B.   False   C.   Can't tell

86. According to the passage, at this point of time, amongst the educated:
A.   A vocal majority believe that dreams come from somewhere outside the dreamer.
B.   A small minority believes that dreams come from the dreamer alone.
C.   The majority accepts that a dreamer's dream is his or her own psychical act.
D.   A vocal minority believes dreams are the direct products of angels and devils.

87. With a dream:
A.   Images seemingly logically dictate feelings.
B.   Events happen which are pleasant to waking thought.
C.   Only boring things occur that are often too dull to be remembered.
D.   There are relationships between images and feelings that would appear illogical to the awake mind.

88. The passage wonders about the significance of individual dreams.
A. True   B. False   C. Can't tell

89. Which of the following statements is supported by the above passage:
A. There is a definite link between the waking and dreaming self.
B. Human society has never had a hypothesis to explain dreams that has satisfied them.
C. A memory of a dream may be untrustworthy.
D. The origin of the dream has been scientifically sourced.

SET 19

Most of the colonists who lived along the American seaboard in 1750 were the descendants of immigrants who had come in fully a century before; after the first settlements there had been much less fresh immigration than many latter-day writers have assumed. According to Prescott F. Hall, "the population of New England ... at the date of the Revolutionary War ... was produced out of an immigration of about 20,000 persons who arrived before 1640," and we have Franklin's authority for the statement that the total population of the colonies in 1751, then about 1,000,000, had been produced from an original immigration of less than 80,000. Even at that early day, indeed, the colonists had begun to feel that they were distinctly separated, in culture and customs, from the mother-country and there were signs of the rise of a new native aristocracy, entirely distinct from the older aristocracy of the royal governors' courts. The enormous difficulties of communication with England helped to foster this sense of separation. The round trip across the ocean occupied the better part of a year, and was hazardous and expensive; a colonist who had made it was a marked man—as Hawthorne said, "the petit maître of the colonies." Nor was there any very extensive exchange of ideas, for though most of the books read in the colonies came from England, the great majority of the colonists, down to the middle of the century, seem to have read little save the Bible and biblical commentaries, and in the native literature of the time one seldom comes upon any reference to the English authors who were glorifying the period of the Restoration and the reign of Anne.

90. Over half of the 1750 colonists that lived on the American seaboard had genetic links to immigrants who had arrived a century ago.

A. True   B. False   C. Can't tell

91. Which of the following statements is supported by the above passage:

A. According to Hall, America's population at the date of the Revolutionary war could be entirely traced back to 20,000 immigrants.

B. The population in the 1751 colonies was over ten times the original immigration that moved there.

C. According to Hall, in 1751 the population in the American colonies was one million.

D. According to Hall, 80,000 people led to a population of 1,000,000.

92. According to the passage, the new aristocracy that existed in the colonies was:

A. Similar to the England's.

B. Similar to European aristocratic systems in general.

C. Not based in royal governors' courts.

D. Not based on genetic lines.

93. Most of the books on board ships were Bibles and Biblical commentaries.

A. True   B. False   C. Can't tell

94. Which of these is **NOT** given as a reason for poor communications with England:

A. Travel between America and England was costly.

B. The English saw the early colonists as backwards.

C. Travel between America and England was slow.

D. Travel between America and England was dangerous.

SET 20

In discussing Russia's role in the past World War, it is customary to cite the losses sustained by the Russian Army, losses running into many millions. There is no doubt that Russia's sacrifices were great, and it is just as true that her losses were greater than those sustained by any of the other Allies. Nevertheless, these sacrifices are by far not the only standard of measurement of Russia's participation in this gigantic struggle. Russia's role must be gauged, first of all, by the efforts made by the Russian Army to blast the German war plans during the first years of the War, when neither America, nor Italy, nor Romania were among the belligerents, and the British Army was still in the process of formation.

[Secondly], and this is the main thing, the role played by the Russian Army must be considered also in this respect that the strenuous campaign waged by Russia, with her 180 millions of inhabitants, for three years against Germany, Austro-Hungary and Turkey, sapped the resources of the enemy and thereby made possible the delivery of the final blow. This weakening of the powers of the enemy by Russia was already bound at various stages of the War to facilitate correspondingly the various operations of the Allies. Therefore, at the end of the War, three years of effort on the part of Russia had devoured the enemy's forces, enabling the Allies to finally crush the enemy. The final catastrophe of the Central Powers was the direct consequence of the offensive of the Allies in 1918, but Russia made possible this collapse to a considerable degree, having effected, in common with the others, the weakening of Germany, and having consumed during the three years of strenuous fighting countless reserves, forces, and resources of the Central Powers.

Could Germany have won the War? A careful analysis of this question brings home the conviction that Germany was very close to victory, and that it required unusual straining of efforts on the part of France and Russia to prevent Germany from "winning out.

95. According to the passage, Russia's greatest contribution to the War was?
A. Contributing more sacrifices than any other ally.
B. Blasting the German war plans during the first years of the War.
C. Consuming countless reserves, forces and resources of the Germans.
D. Sapping the resources of Germany, Austro-Hungary and Turkey for 3 years.

96. How many countries were Russian allies?
A. 2.   B. 3.   C. 4.   D. 5.

97. Russia was the main country fighting against Germany in the early years of the War?
A. True.   B. False.   C. Can't tell.

98. The War was won by?
A. Germany running out of resources.
B. The offensive drive of the Allies.
C. The arrival of America.
D. Turkey and Austro-Hungary changing sides.

99. If it were not for Russia, Germany would have won the war?
A. True.   B. False.   C. Can't tell

QUANTITATIVE LITERACY (QL)

THE BASICS

The Quantitative Literacy subtest tests your ability to quickly interpret data and perform relevant calculations upon them. There are different types of question you can be asked, but all involve interpreting a numerical data source and performing calculations. This is all about testing your natural ability with numbers, how easily you understand numbers and how well you can make calculations based upon new data. Common sources include food menus, timetables, sales figures, surveys, conversion tables and more.

Preparation

Practice common question styles
Be especially comfortable with things like bus and rail timetables, sales figures, surveys, converting units and working with percentage changes in both directions. Likewise, be sharp on your simple arithmetic – it might seem basic, but a good knowledge of times tables will save you a lot of time. Even if you're not answering questions, you can hone your skills by practicing reading charts, graphs and tables quickly.

Familiarise yourself with the format of diagrams
Working through plenty of practice questions will help here, as you'll see similar questions coming up again and again. Commonly you will need to use timetables, data tables and different types of graphs to answer questions. Make sure you are comfortable with these styles of questions.

When looking at an unfamiliar diagram, a clear approach will help you quickly grasp what it shows. Candidates who let the time pressure stop them from properly interpreting the data are much more likely to lose marks. Avoid this common pitfall by following our approach below to quickly read complex data.

Table

Graph

Read any rubric or instructions	**Read any rubric or instructions**
Look at the Headings	**Look at the Axes**
Look at the Units	**Look at the Units**
Look at the data - are there any obvious patterns?	**Look at the plot - are there any obvious trends??**

Mental Speed

The main challenge in most questions is finding the right data and selecting the appropriate calculation to perform, rather than the actual calculation itself. However, time is tight so you should be confident with addition, subtraction, multiplication, division, as well as working out percentages, fractions and ratios. There are some good websites and apps to practice quick-fire mental arithmetic – using these you can quickly refresh these essential skills.

Answering Questions

Estimation

Estimation can be very helpful, particularly when the answers are significantly different. If, for instance, answers are an order of magnitude or more away from each other, you can ignore the fine print of the numbers and still get the right answer. If it's a particularly complicated calculation, quickly ask yourself roughly what answer you are expecting. Another important use of estimation is to generate educated guesses if you're short on time. A quick glance or simplified sum might help you eliminate a few answers in only seconds, boosting the chance your guess is correct.

Flagging for review

Flagging for review is so quick and easy, it can always be a useful tool. If you're finding a question difficult, or you've decided it is likely to take too long to solve, put a guess (or quick estimation if possible), flag for review and move on. This allows you to revisit the question at the end if there's time whilst using your time more efficiently elsewhere. When doing this you should make an initial guess, as this ensures you have at least a chance of being correct if you don't have enough time to come back again.

Read the question first

If the data looks complex, it makes sense to look at the question first before beginning to interpret the data. Just like long questions in the AL section of the NBT, it can take a few moments to interpret the data provided. By reading the question first, you focus your mind, giving you a better focus to approach the data with and ensuring you only spend time analysing data you actually need to work from.

Top tip! Don't spend too long on any one question. In the time it takes to answer one hard question, you could gain three times the marks by answering three easier questions. *Make the most of every second!*

Example:

The following table shows a bank's currency conversion rates between different currencies, with the purchasing currency being listed on the left and the purchased currency being listed across the top. The bank charges a flat fee commission rate of £2.50 on all transactions.

	EUR	AUD	USD	GBP	SAR	INR
EUR	1.00	1.41	1.12	0.75	17.12	69
USD	0.89	1.26	1.00	0.67	15.34	62
GBP	1.33	1.88	1.48	1.00	19.66	92
AUD	0.71	1.00	0.80	0.53	10.15	49

Peter is travelling to Australia next summer and requires AUD. Using the given currency conversion rates, how much will it cost him in GBP, to the nearest pound, to purchase 650 AUD?

A. £343
B. £346
C. £348
D. £1,220
E. £1,224

These answers are in two very different ranges. A quick estimation will narrow down from five to either two or three possible options

Answer: C

This question is assessing your ability to convert, in this case using currency, but may be using different units of area or such like. Again, it is important to read the question closely to ensure you use the correct currencies, and do not miss the commission rate. Find the row which states the currencies per 1GBP, in this case this is the third row. These are the conversion rates you should be using for your calculation. In this question it is worth simply noting that the amount in GBP will be less than the amount in AUD, as each 1GBP buys you towards 2AUD. This will be useful to check you have converted with the figures in the correct order, as the final answer you get should be less than 650AUD. It is also necessary to look at what currency the commission rate is in. As it is stated in GBP, the easiest way is to convert and then take off the commission rate. This will save you time as it is not necessary to make a further calculation of converting the commission rate to AUD.

When writing your working it is essential to write the currency each value is in as to not get confused. This is the case for any question which requires conversion between different units.

Convert 650 AUD to GBP: 650 ÷1.88 (conversion rate GBP to AUD) = £345.74

Price after commission fee 345.74 + 2.50 (commission fee) = £348.24

The question asks for the answer to the nearest pound, therefore final answer = £348

QUANTITATIVE LITERACY QUESTIONS

SET I

The country of Ecunemia has a somewhat complicated tax code. There are four states that make up Ecunemia: Asteria, Bolovia, Casova and Derivia. Each state has its own tax code, including different tax rates on different items. The table below represents the tax a **customer** has to pay when they purchase an item from a store.

	Asteria	Bolovia	Casova	Derivia
Clothes	10%	15%	10%	10%
Food	5%	0%	10%	0%
Imports from other states	20%	5%	10%	15%

The customer must add the tax onto the advertised purchase price. In the case of an item falling into multiple categories (for example, in the case of Imported Food) the higher tax rate is paid and the lower rate is ignored.

Question 1:

A shopper visits a certain supermarket. Without tax, the shopper spends $50 on food, $30 on clothes and nothing on imported items. She spends $88 in total. Which state is this supermarket in?

A. Asteria   B. Bolovia   C. Casova   D. Derivia

Question 2:

Someone runs a supplier in Bolovia, supplying supermarkets in each state in Ecumenia. Each year they supply each state with 250 items of clothing, which the supermarket sells for $40 (including tax), and the supplier gets all of this revenue, minus the tax paid. A competitor in Asteria goes out of business, and this supplier has the opportunity to buy the manufacturing plant for $20,000, and transfer to this state.

58

If the supplier purchases the site, and moves to Asteria, how many years will it take to make back the cost of purchasing the site?

A. 5 years   B. 12 years   C. 23 years   D. 26 years

Question 3:

John goes into a store and spends $100. Of this, $12 is tax. Which of the following is possible?

A. He shopped in Asteria and bought no imported goods.
B. He shopped in Casova.
C. He shopped in Derivia and bought at least $50 of food (excluding tax).
D. He shopped in Bolovia and spent $10 on imported goods (excluding tax).

Question 4:

Sibella is on a road trip through Ecunemia, driving through different states. On the journey she buys $100 of the finest Asterian ham, $30 of the finest Bolovian caviar, a $10 case of Casovan orange juice and spends $100 on a Derivian dress (all of these prices without tax). Which of the following cannot have been the total amount Sibella spent, including tax?

A. $256   B. $264   C. $273   D. $288

SET 2

As a probe drops through the ocean, the pressure it experiences increases. For every 10 metres the probe drops down, the pressure it experiences increases by 10,000 Pascals (Pa).

Question 5:

A particular probe can survive 200 pounds per square inch without incurring damage. Given that the conversion factor between these units is 7000 Pa = 1 pound per square inch and assuming that pressure at sea level is 0 Pascals, how deep can the probe drop into the ocean without incurring damage?

A. 14 m   B. 140 m   C. 1.4 km   D. 14 km

59

Question 6:
A different probe is dropped into the ocean and falls downward. This probe can withstand 300,000 Pa of pressure without breaking. A model of the effect of the fluid states that the object's depth in the fluid is $d = \frac{1}{2}\sqrt{(t^3)}$, where d is depth in metres and t is time in seconds. How long will it take for this probe to break?

A. 65 seconds   C. 75 seconds
B. 71 seconds   D. 78 seconds.

SET 3
The fictional drug Cordrazine is used to treat four separate conditions. The following table gives the amount of drug used in each case to treat each condition, written in the form x mg/kg: i.e. for every kilogram you weigh, you take x mg of the drug. The recommended course for the drug is also listed, in the form of number of times a day and how many weeks you need to take the drug.

Condition	Dosage	Course
Black Trump Virus	4 mg/kg	3 times daily for 4 weeks
Swamp Fever	3 mg/kg	Once daily, 1 week
Yellow Tick	1 mg/kg	2 times daily for 12 weeks
Red Rage	5 mg/kg	2 times daily, 3 weeks

Question 7:
Over the course of treatment, John, an 80 kg male, takes 26.88 grams of the drug. Which disease was he prescribed the drug for?

A. Black Trump Virus   C. Yellow Tick
B. Swamp Fever   D. Red Rage

Question 8:
Carol is a 60 kg female who is prescribed the drug (precisely and at different times) three times in one year. Two of the cases are for Yellow Tick. In total she takes 40.32 grams of the drug. Which was the third disease she was prescribed the drug for?

A. Black Trump Virus   C. Yellow Tick
B. Swamp Fever   D. Red Rage

Question 9:

Clarence takes the drug twice in his life. Once he takes it for Swamp Fever at age 18, when he weighs 80 kg, and he takes it later in life at age 40 for Black Trump Virus, when he weighs 110 kg. What is the ratio of the amount he takes each time?

A. 1:23   B. 1:22   C. 1:21   D. 1:20

Question 10:

Danny has liver disease. His system cannot cope with more than 15.5 grams of Cordrazine every 4 weeks. Danny has a medical condition usually treated with Cordrazine, but doctors have advised him to not complete a course of the treatment, as he would exceed the dose that his system is able to cope with. Which of the following statements is possible?

A. Danny suffers from Red Rage and weighs 75 kg.
B. Danny suffers from Swamp Fever and weighs 100 kg.
C. Danny suffers from Black Trump and weighs 45 kg.
D. Danny suffers from Yellow Tick and weighs 75 kg.

Question 11:

Eileen has kidney failure. Her system cannot cope with more than 10 grams of Cordrazine every 4 weeks. She suffers from Red Rage, but doctors have recommended she does not use Cordrazine to treat it, as this would exceed the 10 g dosage her system can cope with. Which of the following weights is the minimum that would support this recommendation?

A. 40.34 kg   B. 42.53 kg   C. 45.81 kg   D. 47.62 kg

SET 4

A bakery sells four varieties of cakes. The cakes contain the following ingredients:

	Sponge (520g)	Madeira (825g)	Pound (710g)	Chocolate (885g)
Flour (g)	125	250	150	200
Butter (g)	125	175	185	175
Egg (g)	120	180	180	120
Milk (g)	25	45	45	150
Sugar (g)	125	175	150	200
Cocoa (g)	-	-	-	40

Question 12:

Which cake contains the highest proportion of flour?

A. Sponge   C. Pound

B. Madeira   D. Chocolate.

Question 13:

The cake recipes are scaled up for a large order. One cake weighs 2.6 kg and contains 625 g of flour. What variety of cake is it?

A. Sponge   C. Pound

B. Madeira   D. Chocolate

Question 14:

Eliza is having a wedding and wants to produce a 4-tiered wedding cake. She wishes each tier to be of different size, and scaled such that that the bottom cake is 50% heavier than normal (e.g. the cake contains 50% more ingredients), the second cake is 25% heavier than normal, the third cake is 10% heavier than normal and the top cake is normal-sized, where each cake is of the same type.

Which of the following is a possible weight of sugar for the cake (rounded to 2 s.f.)?

A. 940 g   B. 970 g   C. 1,000 g   D. 1,030 g

Question 15:
It is known that flour costs £0.55 per 1.5 kg and sugar costs £0.70 per 1 kg. Which of the following is the closest to the cost ratio of flour to sugar in a Madeira cake?

A. 1:2   B. 3:4   C. 4:5   D. 5:6

Question 16:
Milk costs £0.44 per kilogram and flour costs £0.55 per 1.5 kg. What is the cost ratio of flour to milk in a chocolate cake?

A. 1:1   B. 2:3   C. 8:7   D. 10:9

SET 5
The Kryptos Virus is particularly virulent. The infection rate is dependent upon the gender of the recipient. A random sample of 100 men and 100 women are taken from a population and tested for the Kryptos virus using Test A. The results of Test A are displayed below:

	Men	Women
Have virus	45	63
Do not have virus	55	37

Question 17:
What percentage of people tested have the virus?

A. 45%   B. 54%   C. 55%   D. 63%

Question 18:
A population of 231,768 is divided: 53% women, 47% men. Use the data in the table to estimate the number of people in the population that have the Kryptos virus. Assume that the infection rates in each gender will be the same as for the sample population in Test A. Which of the following is the number of people expected to be infected with Kryptos virus in this population?

A. 123,587   B. 123,589   C. 125,541   D. 126,406

Question: 19

3/9 of the men and 5/7 of the women testing positive for Kryptos in Test A have visited the city of Atlantis. Which of the following is the correct percentage of people in the test group testing positive for Kryptos who have **NOT** visited Atlantis?

A. 40%   B. 44%   C. 50%   D. 55%

Question 20:

It is known that Test A is not always correct. Test B is a more accurate test. The 45 men who tested positive for the Kryptos virus using Test A were then re-tested with Test B - only 20 tested positive. Assuming the same proportion of men and women experienced false positive results with Test A, how many women in the test group do we expect to actually have the Kryptos virus?

A. 20   B. 28   C. 35   D. 42

Question 21:

It is decided the women who tested positive under test A should be retested using test B. This time 29 women test positive for the Kryptos Virus. Considering both the men and women tested, what percentage of people who tested positive in Test A also tested positive in Test B (to the nearest whole number)?

A. 40%   B. 45%   C. 50%   D. 55%

SET 6

A business has 3 warehouses and 3 stores. Each warehouse can ship to each store, and the following table shows the flat rate cost, in South African Rand (R), of the business sending a truck from the warehouse to the store.

	Store 1	Store 2	Store 3
Warehouse A	100	190	530
Warehouse B	120	180	600
Warehouse C	140	200	450

Question 22:
Currently the businesses strategy is to send material from Warehouse A to store 2, from Warehouse B to store 3 and from Warehouse C to store 1. One truck is sufficient for a day's delivery. What is the daily cost of this plan?
A. 850 R B. 930 R C. 970 R D. 1,030 R

Question 23:
The store wishes to optimize their shipping costs by sending material from Warehouse C to store 3, noticing that the delivery cost is lower. They then choose the two other options that save the most money. What percentage saving is achieved by this strategy relative to the strategy in the previous question (to the nearest whole number)?
A. 18% B. 20% C. 22% D. 24%

SET 7
The table below shows the number of books sold by a bookshop in one day:

	Below 18	Above 18
Non-Fiction	12	30
Horror	50	45
Sci-Fi/Fantasy	23	90
Other Fiction	103	159

Question 24:
The shop also ran an author's visit event in the evening in which 106 people purchased the author's book. These books are **NOT** counted in the above table. What proportion of the books sold on this particular day were sold at the author's visit event (to the nearest whole number)?
A. 13% B. 17% C. 21% D. 25%

Question 25:
Non-fiction books cost, on average, £10, and fiction books cost, on average, £6. What percentage of the shop's revenue (excluding the author's visit event) came from non-fiction books?
A. 10% B. 13% C. 19% D. 23%

Question 26:

Assume that the shop makes this number of sales of each type of book every day. One week, the shop adopts a new marketing strategy and markets non-fiction books more heavily. The result is that the number of non-fiction sales double during this week, but all of the other book sales stay in line with previous sales. How much does the shop earn this week?

A. £24,250   B. £25,620   C. £26,950   D. £27,890

Question 27:

The following week, the shop decides to market the horror books more heavily, resulting in the sales of horror books doubling, and the sales of non-fiction books returning to the normal level. How much does the shop's income increase this week compared to the non-fiction marketing week? Sales of all other books can be assumed to be the same as un-marketed weeks.

A. 1%   B. 2%   C. 3%   D. 4%

SET 8

The following table shows the taxing structure for Italian city hotels:

City	Tax
Venice	1 euro per star per room per night. Rooms with children under 16 are tax exempt.
Rome	Per person, per night: 5 euros for 3 star, 6 euros for 4 star, 7 euros for 5 star, up to a maximum of ten nights worth, after which no tax is charged. Rooms with children under age 10 are tax exempt.
Padua	Per person, per night: 2 euros for 3 star or below, 3 euros for 4 star or above. Rooms with children under 16 are tax exempt.
Siena	2 euros per person per night in high season, 1 euro per person per night in low season. Rooms with children under 12 are tax exempt.

Unless specifically mentioned, assume that all of the people below are aged 18 or over.

Question 28:
A family goes on a tour of Italy in the High season. They are 2 adults and 2 children, aged 9 and 13. They spend two nights in each of Venice, Rome, Padua and Siena. They stay in 3 star hotels for the entire trip, and have two rooms (an adult room and a child room). How much tax do they pay for their trip?
A. EUR 35   B. EUR 56   C. EUR 60   D. EUR 65

Question 29:
Claude is comparing cities. He can either spend 7 nights in Rome in a 4 star hotel, or 8 nights in Padua in a 5 star hotel. Which of the following is the ratio between the tax he pays in Rome and the tax he pays in Padua?
A. 8:3   B. 7:4   C. 6:2   D. 1:4

Question 30:
Alice goes on a trip for 2 days to Venice in a 3 star hotel and for 3 days to Padua in a 4 star hotel. What is the percentage more tax she pays in Padua relative to Venice?
A. 25%   B. 50%   C. 75%   D. 100%

Question: 31
How long does Reuben have to stay in a 4 star hotel in Rome so that the tax would be less than or equal to the tax he incurs if staying the same length of time in a 4 star hotel in Padua?
A. 10 days   B. 15 days   C. 20 days   D. 25 days

SET 9

The graph below shows the total amount of CO_2 (in Tonnes) emitted by the country Aissur in each year from 2000 onwards.

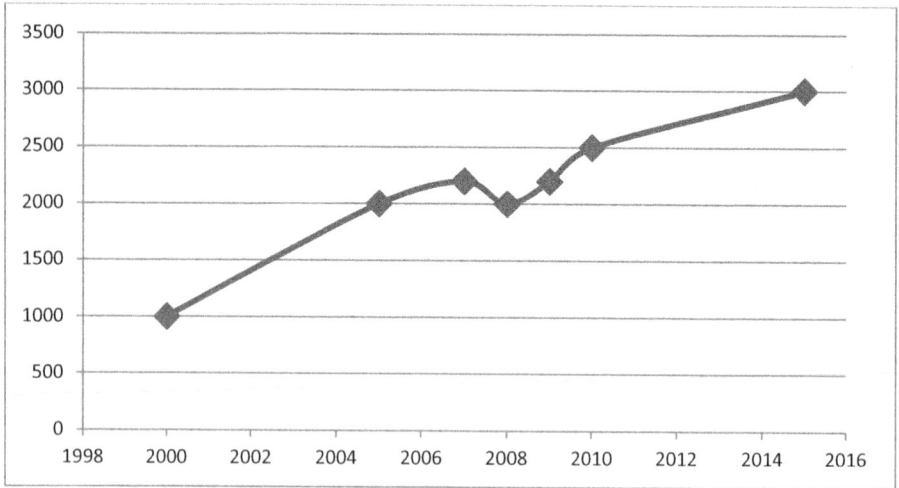

Question 32:

What was the rate of increase of CO_2 emissions between 2000 and 2005?

A. 250 Tonnes/year

B. 225 Tonnes/year

C. 200 Tonnes/year

D. 100 Tonnes/year

Question 33:

The economic crash of 2008 caused global CO_2 emissions to decrease due to a decrease in industrial output. How much less CO_2 was emitted in the year 2010 compared to if emissions had continued to rise at the same rate seen from 2000 to 2005?

A. 500 Tonnes

B. 750 Tonnes

C. 1,000 Tonnes

D. 2,500 Tonnes

Question 34:

What is the percentage increase in CO_2 emissions from 2005 to 2015?

A. 25%   B. 33%   C. 50%   D. 150

Question 35:

In 2015, the government of Aissur voted on a new energy bill. The bill seeks to reduce the rate of CO_2 increase over the past 5 years by 50% over the next 5 years, and keep the increase at this level thereafter. If the new energy bill is successful in meeting its aims, how much CO_2 will be saved by the end of 2020 relative to the 2010 – 2015 trend continuing?

A. 200 Tonnes

B. 250 Tonnes

C. 500 Tonnes

D. 750 Tonnes

SET 10

4 sets of 300 volunteers take part in a clinical trial for a new drug, which is aimed at reducing the effects of asthma. The responses received are recorded below.

Group	Positive	Negative	No Effect
1	75%	20%	5%
2	65%	30%	5%
3	70%	15%	15%
4	55%	25%	20%

Question 36:

How many people reacted positively overall?

A. 135   B. 265   C. 523   D. 795

Question 37:

How many more people reacted negatively from set 2 compared to set 3?

A. 15   B. 33   C. 45   D. 56

Question 38:

What proportion of those tested overall reacted negatively?

A. 21%   B. 23%   C. 26%   D. 28%

After modifications to the drug, a new survey of 300 volunteers was taken. The results of this are shown below:

Group	Positive	Negative	No Effect
5	82%	15%	3%

Question 39:
What was the percentage increase in the success rate (i.e. the percentage of people reacting positively) in the 5th group compared to the first 4 groups?
A. 7.81%   B. 15.75%   C. 17.93%   D. 23.77%

Question 40:
Across all groups, including group 5, how many people reacted negatively to the drug?
A. 275   B. 315   C. 355   D. 380

SET II
A muffin recipe calls for ingredients in the amounts listed in the table below:

Ingredient	Density	Amount
Flour	600 gram/dm³	2 cups
Sugar	850 gram/dm³	1 cup
Milk	1050 gram/dm³	½ cup
Butter	950 gram/dm³	4 tablespoons

1 cup = 2.5 decilitres (dl); 1 tablespoon = 15 millilitres (ml); 1 cubic decimetre (dm³) = 1 litre

Question 41:
How many cups of ingredients are called for overall by the recipe (to 2 decimal places)?
A. 3.54   B. 3.66   C. 3.74   D. 3.82   E. 3.86

Question 42:
What weight ratio of milk to butter does the recipe call for (to 1 decimal place)?
A. 2.3:1   B. 2.7:1   C. 3.1:1   D. 3.4:1   E. 3.9:1

Question 43:
Jane wants to use only a ½ cup measure for baking. What is the smallest number of cups of flour she would need for it to be possible to measure all required ingredients in ½ cups?
A. 2   B. 10   C. 25   D. 30   E. 50

Question 44:
To make pancakes, the amount of flour and milk are reversed. What is the average density of pancake batter, assuming that there are no interactions that change the densities of the individual ingredients when they are mixed?

A. 930 grams/dm³   D. 1,070 grams/dm³
B. 970 grams/dm³   E. 1,100 grams/dm³
C. 1,050 grams/dm³

Question 45:
If Peter wanted to make 10 muffins weighing 100 grams each, how much butter would he need to 1 decimal place? Assume that the finished product weighs the same as the initial dough.
A. 55.1 grams   C. 70.7 grams   E. 81.3 grams
B. 62.3 grams   D. 76.4 grams

Question 46:
When Peter's ten 100 gram muffins are done, assuming no losses to cooking, what percentage of the weight will be made up by flour, to the nearest whole number?
A. 35 %   B. 39 %   C. 43 %   D. 46 %   E. 52 %

SET 12

New ocean crust is formed at spreading ridges. The area of the crust formed is dependent on temperature. The volume of crust formed in a given time interval depends on the **crust cross sectional area** and on the spreading rate (the rate at which newly formed crust moves away from the spreading ridge, an independent variable).

The relationship between **crust volume** formed in a time interval, **cross sectional area** and **spreading rate** is:

Crust volume per time = cross sectional area x spreading rate

The table below gives the crustal cross sectional area, spreading rate and temperature at Locations A-D:

	A	B	C	D
Cross Sectional Area (km²)	10	20	30	40
Spreading rate (mm/year)	150	20	100	50
Temperature (°C)	1300	1400	1500	1600

Question 47:

Assuming that the trends in this table can be reliably extrapolated, at which temperature would the crust volume formed in a year be expected to be 0 km³?

A. 1,200 °C   C. 1,600 °C   E. 2,000 °C
B. 1,400 °C   D. 1.800 °C

Question 48:

If the temperature at Location A increased by 50%, what would be the spreading rate?

A. 25 mm/year   C. 100 mm/year   E. 225 mm/year
B. 50 mm/year   D. 150 mm/year

Question 49:
What volume of crust is formed in a year at Location B?
A. 400 m³
B. 400 km³
C. 40,000 km³
D. 400,000 m³
E. 560,000 km³

Question 50:
If the spreading rates of Locations A and C were exchanged, what would be the ratio of crust volume formed at the two locations each year (to 1 decimal place)?
A. 1:1.0   B. 1:3.3   C. 1:4.5   D. 1:5.6   E. 1:6.0

Question 51:
If the same crustal volume was produced in the same amount of time at 2 locations, E with temperature 1300 °C and F with temperature 1450 °C, how many percent faster/slower was the spreading rate at location E than F?
A. 250 % faster
B. 25 % slower
C. 400 % faster
D. 40 % slower
E. 500 % faster

Question 52:
If the temperature at Location D was decreased by 10%, what would be the crustal volume formed in 3 years?
A. 2,000 m³
B. 2,000 km³
C. 3,200 km³
D. 3, 200,000 m³
E. 3, 600,000,000,000,000 mm³

SET 13

A new drug to treat vision problems in diabetics is tested on volunteers. It is also tested on control groups of diabetics without vision problems and healthy volunteers with or without vision problems. Some volunteers are given one inactive placebo pill which they are told is the drug. There are the same number of people in each group testing either the drug or placebo, as indicated below.

The table below shows the number of volunteers in Groups A-D who self-reported improved vision and their measured average accuracy reading letters before and after taking the drug or a placebo.

	Group A		Group B		Group C		Group D	
	Drug	Placebo	Drug	Placebo	Drug	Placebo	Drug	Placebo
Number Improved	15	9	8	6	9	7	7	8
Accuracy Before (%)	27	27	60	60	29	29	68	68
Accuracy After (%)	36	31	66	61	31	32	70	70

Group A: 50 diabetics with vision problems (25 in each group)
Group B: 46 diabetics without vision problems (23 in each group)
Group C: 44 healthy volunteers with vision problems (22 in each group)
Group D: 48 healthy volunteers without vision problems (24 in each group)

Question 53:

What is the average percentage of participants who self-report vision improvements after receiving an inactive pill to the nearest percent?

A. 26 %   B. 31 %   C. 32 %   D. 33 %   E. 36 %

Question 54:
By what ratio is visual accuracy in reading letters increased by the drug in diabetics with poor sight relative to healthy volunteers with poor sight (to 2 decimal places)?

A. 1:0.78   C. 4.21:1   E. 4.83:1
B. 3.50:1   D. 4.50:1

Question 55:
If there are 10 women in Group A and their average accuracy was 45 % after receiving the drug, what was the average accuracy of the men in the group after receiving the drug?

A. 16 %   B. 27 %   C. 30 %   D. 36 %   E. 41 %

	Group A		Group B		Group C		Group D	
	Drug	Placebo	Drug	Placebo	Drug	Placebo	Drug	Placebo
Number Improved	15	9	8	6	9	7	7	8
Accuracy Before (%)	27	27	60	60	29	29	68	68
Accuracy After (%)	36	31	66	61	31	32	70	70

Group A: 50 diabetics with vision problems (25 in each group)
Group B: 46 diabetics without vision problems (23 in each group)
Group C: 44 healthy volunteers with vision problems (22 in each group)
Group D: 48 healthy volunteers without vision problems (24 in each group)

Question 56:
If the general population has 100 000 diabetics with vision problems, how many of these people would be expected to self-report improvements in their vision because of the effects of the drug?

A. 24,000 people   C. 36,000 people   E. 96,000 people
B. 32,000 people   D. 60,000 people

Question 57:

When the drug dose was doubled, the placebo groups showed no change in numbers or accuracy, but the number of Group A volunteers who reported improved vision jumped to 18. Assuming that drug effectiveness is dose dependent, what percent of volunteers in Group A taking the drug would be expected to self-report improved vision if the dose was tripled?

A. 54.0 %　　　　　　　　C. 84.0 %　　　　　　　　E. 100.0 %
B. 72.0 %　　　　　　　　D. 90.0 %

Question 58:

Which of the following statements is supported by the data in the table?
A. The placebo is more effective than the drug.
B. The drug acts to improve vision in diabetics and healthy volunteers.
C. Volunteers who see well are more motivated to improve vision than those with vision problems.
D. Thinking you have taken a drug to improve vision improves your vision.
E. The data are inconclusive.

SET 14

Dave weighs 200 pounds and has a Basal Metabolic Rate (BMR) of 2000 calories. Elizabeth weighs 140 pounds and has a BMR of 1500 calories. The table below shows the calorific value of the foods they eat:

	Cereal	Sandwich	Apple	Chocolate	Lasagna	Chicken	Vegetables
Calories	400	500	100	350	700	250	200

To lose one pound of fat requires a 3500 calorie deficit, obtained by eating fewer calories than the BMR or burning calories by exercising.

Running burns 5 calories per hour per pound you weigh at any running speed.

Cycling burns calories according to the following relationship, where M is mph cycling speed:

Calories burned per mile = 50 calories + (5 calories x (M-10))

Question 59:
Dave wants his workout to take one hour on a 5 mile track. What is the maximum number of calories he can burn by running or cycling?
A. Burn 125 calories running
B. Burn 125 calories cycling
C. Burn 1,000 calories running
D. Burn 1,000 calories cycling
E. Burn 1,250 calories running

Question 60:
Dave doesn't want to eat less than his BMR and can only run for 30 minutes a day, but cycles 20 miles every day in an hour. How long will it take him to lose 10 pounds?
A. 5 days
B. 7 days
C. 10 days
D. 14 days
E. 30 days

Question 61:
Elizabeth and Dave both want to lose 10% of their body weight without dieting or cycling. What is the ratio of minutes a day Elizabeth would have to run to those Dave would have to run to achieve their goal at the same time to 1 decimal place?
A. 1:0.5   B. 1:0.7   C. 1:1.0   D. 1:1.4   E. 1:2.0

Question 62:
If Elizabeth eats cereal for breakfast, a sandwich for lunch, chicken and vegetables for dinner and does no exercise, in how many full days will she have reached her goal of 10% weight-loss?
A. 327 days
B. 354 days
C. 372 days
D. 416 days
E. 435 days

Question 63:
If Elizabeth also began cycling 10 miles in 1 hour every day, how much faster would she reach her goal than in question 62?
A. 1.00   B. 2.50   C. 3.00   D. 3.33   E. 4.33

Question 64:

Elizabeth eats one chocolate everyday; 3 times as much chicken as chocolate and twice as much cereal as chicken. If she exchanged these foods with 3 different foods in the table in the same proportions, what is the ratio of her rate of weight change before and after the switch, assuming she is trying to obtain the lowest weight she can?

A. 1:1   B. 1:2   C. 1:5   D. 2:1   E. 5:1

SET 15

The table below shows the production of some agricultural crops in Harvestland in the years 2011-12 and the targets that were earlier set for that growing season.

Crop	Targeted production For 2011-12 (tonnes)	Actual production for 2011-12 (tonnes)	% Increase in production from 2010-11
Food grains	120	100	25
Oil seeds	60	50	25
Sugarcane	50	40	10
Cotton	40	30	20
Jute	25	20	25

Question 65:

The production of food grain (in tonnes) in 2010-11 was:

A. 40   B. 60   C. 80   D. 100

Question 66:

What was the difference in targeted production in 2011-12 and actual production in 2010-11 for oil seeds (in tonnes)?

A. 10   B. 20   C. 30   D. 40

Question 67:

How much more sugarcane should have been produced in order to meet the target in 2011-12 (in tonnes)?

A. 5   B. 10   C. 15   D. 20

Question 68:

What was the combined production of Cotton and Jute in year 2010-11 (in tonnes)?

A. 11   B. 21   C. 31   D. 41

Question 69:

How much more food grain was produced than oil seeds in 2010-11 (in TONNES)?

A. 10   B. 20   C. 30   D. 40

SET 16

The table given below shows the sales volume of four products A, B, C and D manufactured by a company from January to April in the year 2014.

	January	February	March	April
Product A	9,500	10,250	10,500	11,000
Product B	6,500	7,000	7,250	7,500
Product C	3,500	3,750	4,000	4,250
Product D	2,500	3,100	3,500	4,000

Question 70:

In February, sale of product B constituted what percentage of total sales of all 4 products put together?

A. 26%   B. 27%   C. 28%   D. 29%

Question 71:
Which of the following products recorded maximum percentage increase from March to April?

A. Product A

B. Product B

C. Product C

D. Product D

Question 72:
In May 2014, the sales of product C witnessed an increase of 20% over the previous month. The sales of D were the same as those of C. What was the percentage increase in the sales of D in May relative to April?

A. 22.5 %

B. 25.0 %

C. 27.5 %

D. 30.0 %

Question 73:
By what percentage did the combined sales of product A and product C increase from January to April?

A. 17.0 %

B. 17.1 %

C. 17.2 %

D. 17.3 %

Question 74:
Assume a different scenario, that May 2015 witnessed a 20% growth in sales for products A and B, and a 30% growth in sales for products C and D over April values. What was the total sales value in May for all the products combined?

A. 32,925

B. 33,925

C. 34,925

D. 35,925

SET 17
The following table provides partial information about the composition of three different alloys, A, B and C. Each of these alloys contains five different elements: Zinc, Tin, Lead, Copper and Nickel, and no other substances. An alloy, Alloy G, the composition of which is not given in the table, contains alloys A, B, C in the ratio 2:1:3. It is also known that in Alloy G, Tin, Lead and Copper are present in equal quantities.

Alloy	Zinc	Tin	Lead	Copper	Nickel
A	10%	40%			10%
B	25%	15%	50%	5%	5%
C	15%		20%		35%

Question 75:
Find the percentage of Lead in alloy A.

A. 8.33 %   B. 4,16 %   C. 2.70 %   D. 2.08 %

Question 76:
Find the percentage of Tin in alloy C.

A. 31.3 %   B. 15.8 %   C. 10.6 %   D. 7.9 %

Question 77:
An alloy X contains A, B and C in equal proportion. What is the percentage of Zinc in this alloy?

A. 12.50 %   B. 16.67 %   C. 25.00 %   D. 33.33 %

Question 78:
Find the percentage of Tin and Copper combined in alloy C.

A. 15 %   B. 20 %   C. 25 %   D. 30 %

Question 79:
Find the percentage of Tin in alloy G.

A. 11.11 %   B. 21.11 %   C. 31.11 %   D. 41.11 %

Question 80:
How many elements have exactly the same concentration in Alloy G?

A. One   B. Two   C. Three   D. Four

SET 18

In St. Mary College, all students must have at least one device to interact with digital, interactive study materials. There are thirty students who have all three gadgets: Smartphone, tablet and laptop.

All students who only have one of the three gadgets

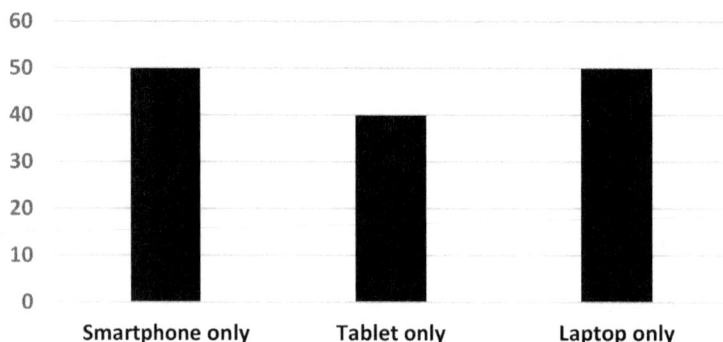

All students who have at least one of the three gadgets

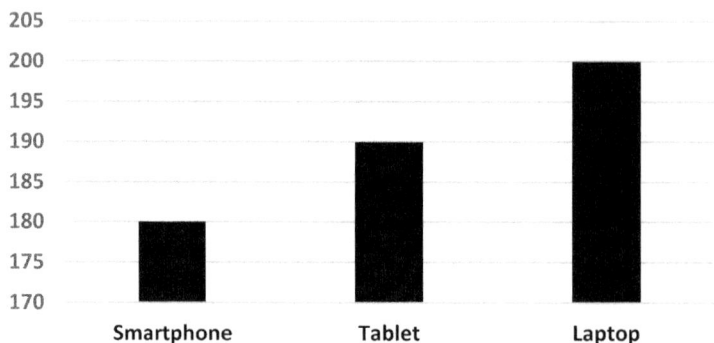

Question 81:

How many students are studying at St. Mary College in total?

A. 325   B. 340   C. 345   D. 350   E. 360

Question 82:
How many students have both a tablet and smartphone but no laptop?
A. 40   B. 45   C. 50   D. 55   E. 65

Question 83:
How many more students have a smartphone than both a tablet and laptop?
A. 80   B. 85   C. 95   D. 100   E. 80

Question 84:
What percentage of all students have both a smartphone and a laptop?
A. 20.5%   C. 23.5%   E. 25.9%
B. 23.1%   D. 25.4%

Question 85:
Five more students come to St. Mary College. Three of the students have both a smartphone and a tablet. Two of the students have a smartphone only. What percentage of all students in the college have a smartphone now?
A. 34%   B. 45%   C. 54%   D. 55%   E. 60%

SET 19

2015 Winter Snowfall (cm)

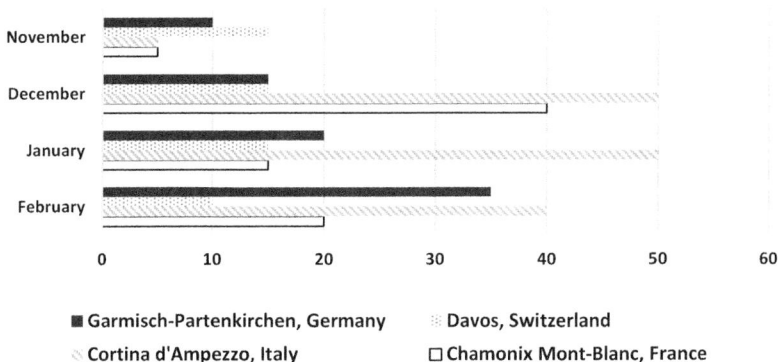

■ Garmisch-Partenkirchen, Germany   Davos, Switzerland
Cortina d'Ampezzo, Italy   ☐ Chamonix Mont-Blanc, France

Question 86:

What was the mean monthly snowfall in cm across Davos and Chamonix Mont-Blanc during winter in 2015?

A. 12.325 cm   C. 19.738 cm   E. 43.123 cm

B. 16.875 cm   D. 26.842 cm

Question 87:

During Winter 2015, where was the average monthly snowfall the highest?

A. Davos   D. Garmisch Partenkirchen

B. Chamonix Mont-Blanc   E. Can't tell

C. Cortina d'Ampezzo

Question 88:

In percentage terms, how much more snow fell in December than in February overall?

A. 8%   B. 12%   C. 14%   D. 20%   E. 22%

Question 89:

In November 2014, 30cm snow fell in the four areas together. In percentage terms, how much more snow fell in November 2015 in the four areas together?

A. 5%   B. 17%   C. 19%   D. 24%   E. 29%

Question 90:

How much snow fell in Cortina d' Ampezzo and Garmisch Partenkirchen in November and February together?

A. 20 cm   C. 60 cm   E. 145 cm

B. 30 cm   D. 90 cm

SET 20

A group of 180 people took part in a perception study and were asked to count how many differences they could spot between two similar pieces of short video footage. The results are given below:

		Age (years)					
		10 to 16	16 to 22	22 to 34	34 to 48	48 to 65	65+
Differences correctly spotted	<5	9	10	10	16	15	19
	5 to 10	7	12	9	8	8	5
	11 to 15	11	8	6	2	8	9
	15+	3	2	0	1	2	0

Question 91:

What percentage of people under the age of 22 spotted more than 10 differences?

A. 31.3%   C. 38.7%   E. 63.2%
B. 33.3%   D. 46.7%

Question 92:

75% of the results for the people who spotted 5 to 10 differences correctly were removed from the study. What percentage of the remaining people aged 16-22 spotted more than 15 differences?

A. 6.3%   C. 8.5%   E. 9.4%
B. 6.9%   D. 8.7%

Question 93:

25% of people who correctly spotted over 10 differences, also *incorrectly* spotted over 10 differences. How many people was this?

A. 11   B. 12   C. 13   D. 14   E. 15

Question 94:

10,000 people aged 48 or older take this test. Using the data, estimate how many spotted fewer than five differences to the nearest 50.

A. 2,300	C. 4,500	E. 5,150
B. 2,900	D. 5,100	F. 5,200

Question 95:

The test is repeated with the same population. The number of 16-34 year olds who spot 11-15 differences increases by 50%. All other age groups experience no change. What is the new ratio between 16-34 year olds and the total number of people in the other age groups who spot 11-15 differences?

A. 1:3	C. 14:44	E. 21:51
B. 4:17	D. 14:51	

SET 21

The pie chart below shows the favourite sports of some high school students. Every student plays only their favourite sport in games lessons. The school has 1300 students, with an exact 50:50 split between boys and girls.

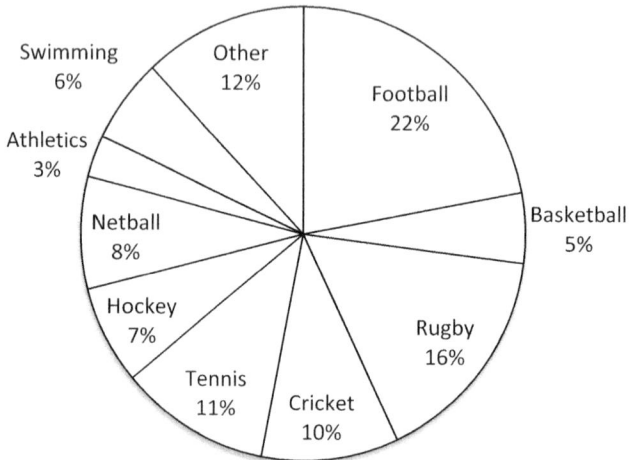

Swimming 6%
Other 12%
Football 22%
Athletics 3%
Netball 8%
Basketball 5%
Hockey 7%
Rugby 16%
Tennis 11%
Cricket 10%

Question 96:

What is the difference between the number of boys that play football and the number that play netball in games lessons?

A. 90   C. 104   E. 182

B. 91   D. 180   F. 286

Question 97:

The senior football teams are picked from the two most senior years – a total of 350 students. Only those whose favourite sport is football play. At least 11 people are needed per team. What is the maximum number of teams that could be made? Assume that the values given in the chart are representative of these years.

A. 4   B. 5   C. 6   D. 7   E. 8

Question 98:

All those whose favourite sport is basketball are boys and all those whose favourite sport is netball are girls. 80% of the basketball boys are invited to play netball. What proportion of the netball-playing population do they then make?

A. 17%   B. 25%   C. 33%   D. 42%   E. 50%

Question 99:

One quarter of students in the *Other* category have a favourite sport which is a ball sport. In the whole school, how many students have a favourite sport which is a ball sport?

A. 39   C. 572   E. 1,183

B. 117   D. 1,066

Question 100:

Only boys play cricket. Only girls play hockey. The gender split for tennis follows that of the school as a whole. How many more boys play cricket or tennis than girls play hockey or tennis?

A. 39   B. 58   C. 59   D. 111   E. 112

SET 22

The number of apples picked by a company per year is given below, along with the quality of the apples. 30% of edible apples are sold as they come. Passable apples and the remaining edible apples are processed into cider.

Apples which are No Good are not used for human consumption, and are instead discarded for animal food.

	1998	1999	2000	2001	2002	2003
Edible	1,100,547	1,398,663	1,563,327	1,443,599	1,763,870	1,931,784
Passable	2,983,411	2,691,553	3,008,941	2,790,456	2,651,399	2,439,012
No Good	400,001	391,747	398,014	568,440	494,309	571,221

Question 101:

What is the percentage increase in the number of apples used for human consumption from 1998 to 2003?

A. 7%   B. 10%   C. 22%   D. 76%   E. 93%

Question 102:

What percentage of all No Good apples was produced in the year most apples could not be used for humans?

A. 11.6%   C. 13.9%   E. 20.2%
B. 11.8%   D. 19.9%

Question 103:

2004 saw a three-fold increase on 2003 in the number of No Good apples. The total number of apples fit for consumption remained the same. What was the difference in number between processed and No Good apples in 2004 to the nearest apple?

A. 2,077,598   C. 2,478,954   E. 2,765,131
B. 2,224,675   D. 2,675,133

Question 104:
The next six-year period saw an overall 20% increase on the period 1998-2003 in the total number of edible apples picked. How many were sold as they came between 2004 and 2009?

A. 3,588,698   C. 3,312,644   E. 2,208,430
B. 3,321,646   D. 2,392,465

Question 105:
Generally, 20 apples give 1 litre of cider. Given that 2004 saw the same number of apples fit for human consumption as 2003, roughly how many litres of cider were produced in 2004?

A. 122,000 l   C. 215,400 l   E. 988,400 l
B. 189,600 l   D. 247,100 l

SET 23
Jen tracks her daily jogs using an app which gives her data on her performance. Her app tells her that her average speed is 5 mph.

Conversion factor: 1 mile = 1.6 km

Question 106:
On wet days, Jen's average speed decreases by 8%. How many kilometres does she cover in 40 minutes?

A. 3.1 km   C. 4.9 km   E. 7.4 km
B. 3.3 km   D. 5.3 km

Question 107:
Jen begins training for a marathon (26 miles). She starts off by trying to complete a marathon over the space of four equally long jogs. Estimate how long each jog is. Assume dry conditions.

A. 42 minutes
B. 46 minutes
C. 1 hour 18 minutes
D. 1 hour 25 minutes
E. 1 hour 30 minutes

Question 108:

After starting marathon training, her average speed decreases to her old wet speed; her average wet speed remaining 8% slower than this. Estimate, therefore, how long it would take her to cover 12km in the rain.

A. 1 hour 38 minutes
B. 1 hour 46 minutes
C. 2 hours 17 minutes
D. 2 hours 37 minutes
E. 2 hours 50 minutes

Question 109:

After bringing her average speeds back to their original values, Jen starts a new regime. She goes on four jogs, each being 50% further than the last. Her first jog is 4km long. How long does the final jog take in dry conditions?

A. 1 hour 8 minutes
B. 1 hour 41 minutes
C. 1 hour 50 minutes
D. 2 hours 9 minutes
E. 2 hours 42 minutes

Question 110:

Lots of training later, Jen completes the marathon in a time of 3hrs 42mins on a dry day. What is the percentage increase in Jen's dry average speed compared to her original one?

A. 7%   B. 12%   C. 41%   D. 52%   E. 53%

SET 24

The table below is a summary of students who signed up for the following courses at St. Mary Grammar School:

Courses	Women	Men
Psychology	10	6
Maths	8	7
Physics	10	15
Programming	4	5
Literature	12	8
History	7	7

Students can take more than one course.

Question 111:
For which course is the ratio of women and men most similar to that of Psychology?

A. Mathematics   C. Programming   E. History
B. Physics   D. Literature

Question 112:
For which course is the ratio of women and men most similar to that of Physics?

A. Mathematics   C. Programming   E. History
B. Psychology   D. Literature

Question 113:
What is the total number of women in St. Mary Grammar School?

A. 34   C. 64   E. Can't Tell
B. 51   D. 145

Question 114:
What is the total proportion of women to men?

A. 0.25   C. 0.96   E. Cannot Say
B. 0.5   D. 1

Question 115:
If three new students arrive at St. Mary Grammar School and they are all women studying Psychology. What is the change in the ratio of women to men studying Psychology?

A. 0.1   B. 0.3   C. 0.5   D. 0.7   E. 1.2

MATHEMATICS (MAT)

The MAT test requires a much broader knowledge of Maths and you're highly advised to revise topics such as algebra, trigonometry and geometry before proceeding further with the practice questions in this book. The questions are designed to be time draining. However, good students sometimes have a habit of making easy questions difficult.

Use the Options:
Some questions may try to overload you with information. When presented with large tables and data, it's essential you look at the answer options so you can focus your mind. This can allow you to reach the correct answer a lot more quickly. Consider the example below:

The table below shows the results of a study investigating antibiotic resistance in staphylococcus populations. A single staphylococcus bacterium is chosen at random from a similar population. Resistance to any one antibiotic is independent of resistance to others.

Antibiotic	Number of Bacteria tested	Number of Resistant Bacteria
Benzyl-penicillin	10^{11}	98
Chloramphenicol	10^9	1200
Metronidazole	10^8	256
Erythromycin	10^5	2

Calculate the probability that the bacterium selected will be resistant to all four drugs.

A. 1 in 10^6 C. 1 in 10^{20} E. 1 in 10^{30}
B. 1 in 10^{12} D. 1 in 10^{25} F. 1 in 10^{35}

Looking at the options first makes it obvious that there is **no need to calculate exact values**- only in powers of 10. This makes your life a lot easier. If you hadn't noticed this, you might have spent time trying to calculate the exact value when it wasn't even being asked for.

In other cases, you may actually be able to use the options to arrive at the solution quicker than if you had tried to solve the question as you normally would. Consider the example below:

A region is defined by the two inequalities: $x - y^2 > 1 \ and \ xy > 1$. Which of the following points is in the defined region?

A. (10,3)   B. (10,2)   C. (-10,3)   D. (-10,2)

Whilst it's possible to solve this question both algebraically or graphically by manipulating the identities, by far **the quickest way is to actually use the options**. Note that options C and violate the second inequality, narrowing down to answer to either A or B. For A: $10 - 3^2 = 1$ and thus this point is on the boundary of the defined region and not actually in the region. Thus the answer is B (as 10-4 = 6 > 1.)

In general, it pays dividends to look at the options briefly and see if they can be help you arrive at the question more quickly. Get into this habit early – it may feel unnatural at first but it's guaranteed to save you time in the long run.

Study key areas
Even confident students can struggle with certain NBT maths topics because they're usually glossed over at school. These include:

Quadratic Formula

The solutions for a quadratic equation in the form $ax^2 + bx + c = 0$ are given by: $x = \frac{-b \pm \sqrt{b^2 - 4ac}}{2a}$

Remember that you can also use the discriminant to quickly see if a quadratic equation has any solutions:

$$If\ b^2 - 4ac < 0: No\ solutions$$
$$If\ b^2 - 4ac = 0: One\ solution$$
$$If\ b^2 - 4ac > 2: Two\ solutions$$

Completing the Square

If a quadratic equation cannot be factorised easily and is in the format $ax^2 + bx + c = 0$ then you can rearrange it into the form $a\left(x + \frac{b}{2a}\right)^2 + [c - \frac{b^2}{4a}] = 0$

This looks more complicated than it is – remember that in the NBT, you're extremely unlikely to get quadratic equations where $a > 1$ and the equation doesn't have any easy factors. This gives you an easier equation: $\left(x + \frac{b}{2}\right)^2 + [c - \frac{b^2}{4}] = 0$ and is best understood with an example.

Consider: $x^2 + 6x + 10 = 0$

This equation cannot be factorised easily but note that: $x^2 + 6x - 10 = (x + 3)^2 - 19 = 0$

Therefore, $x = -3 \pm \sqrt{19}$. Completing the square is an important skill – make sure you're comfortable with it.

Difference between 2 Squares

If you are asked to simplify expressions and find that there are no common factors but it involves square numbers – you might be able to factorise by using the 'difference between two squares'.

For example, $x^2 - 25$ can also be expressed as $(x + 5)(x - 5)$

MATHEMATICS QUESTIONS

Question 1:

Robert has a box of building blocks. The box contains 8 yellow blocks and 12 red blocks. He picks three blocks from the box and stacks them up high. Calculate the probability that he stacks two red building blocks and one yellow building block, in **any** order.

A. $\frac{8}{20}$ C. $\frac{11}{18}$ E. $\frac{12}{20}$

B. $\frac{44}{95}$ D. $\frac{8}{19}$ F. $\frac{35}{60}$

Question 2:

Solve $\frac{3x+5}{5} + \frac{2x-2}{3} = 18$

A. 12.11   C. 13.95   E. 19

B. 13.49   D. 14.2   F. 265

Question 3:

Solve $3x^2 + 11x - 20 = 0$

A. 0.75 and $-\frac{4}{3}$ C. -5 and $\frac{4}{3}$ E. 12 only

B. -0.75 and $\frac{4}{3}$ D. 5 and $\frac{4}{3}$ F. -12 only

Question 4:

Express $\frac{5}{x+2} + \frac{3}{x-4}$ as a single fraction.

A. $\frac{15x-120}{(x+2)(x-4)}$ C. $\frac{8x-14}{(x+2)(x-4)}$ E. 24

B. $\frac{8x-26}{(x+2)(x-4)}$ D. $\frac{15}{8x}$ F. $\frac{8x-14}{x^2-8}$

Question 5:

The value of p is directly proportional to the cube root of q. When p = 12, q = 27. Find the value of q when p = 24.

A. 32

B. 64

C. 124

D. 128

E. 216

F. 1728

Question 6:

Write 72^2 as a product of its prime factors.

A. $2^6 \times 3^4$

B. $2^6 \times 3^5$

C. $2^4 \times 3^4$

D. 2×3^3

E. $2^6 \times 3$

F. $2^3 \times 3^2$

Question 7:

Calculate: $\dfrac{2.302 \; x \; 10^5 + 2.302 \; x \; 10^2}{1.151 \; x \; 10^{10}}$

A. 0.0000202

B. 0.00020002

C. 0.00002002

D. 0.00000002

E. 0.000002002

F. 0.000002002

Question 8:

Given that $y^2 + \mathbf{a}y + \mathbf{b} = (y + 2)^2 - 5$, find the values of **a** and **b**.

	a	b
A	-1	4
B	1	9
C	-1	-9
D	-9	1
E	4	-1
F	4	1

Question 9:

Express $\frac{4}{5} + \frac{m-2n}{m+4n}$ as a single fraction in its simplest form:

A. $\frac{6m+6n}{5(m+4n)}$

C. $\frac{20m+6n}{5(m+4n)}$

E. $\frac{3(3m+2n)}{5(m+4n)}$

B. $\frac{9m+26n}{5(m+4n)}$

D. $\frac{3m+9n}{5(m+4n)}$

F. $\frac{6m+6n}{3(m+4n)}$

Question 10:

A is inversely proportional to the square root of B. When A = 4, B = 25. Calculate the value of A when B = 16.

A. 0.8   C. 5   E. 10
B. 4   D. 6   F. 20

Question 11:

S, T, U and V are points on the circumference of a circle, and O is the centre of the circle.

Given that angle SVU = 89°, calculate the size of the smaller angle SOU.

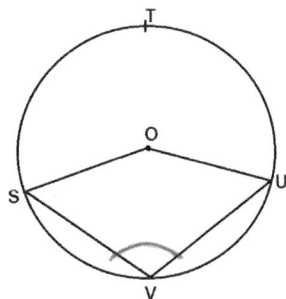

A. 89°   D. 178°
B. 91°   E. 182°
C. 102°   F. 212°

Question 12:

Open cylinder A has a surface area of 8π cm² and a volume of 2π cm³. Open cylinder B is an enlargement of A and has a surface area of 32π cm². Calculate the volume of cylinder B.

A. 2π cm³   C. 10π cm³   E. 16π cm³
B. 8π cm³   D. 14π cm³   F. 32π cm³

Question 13:

Express $\dfrac{8}{x(3-x)} - \dfrac{6}{x}$ in its simplest form.

A. $\dfrac{3x-10}{x(3-x)}$

B. $\dfrac{3x+10}{x(3-x)}$

C. $\dfrac{6x-10}{x(3-2x)}$

D. $\dfrac{6x-10}{x(3+2x)}$

E. $\dfrac{6x-10}{x(3-x)}$

F. $\dfrac{6x+10}{x(3-x)}$

Question 14:

A bag contains 10 balls. 9 of those are white and 1 is black. What is the probability that the black ball is drawn in the tenth and final draw if the drawn balls are not replaced?

A. 0

B. $\dfrac{1}{10}$

C. $\dfrac{1}{100}$

D. $\dfrac{1}{10^{10}}$

E. $\dfrac{1}{362,880}$

Question 15:

Gambit has an ordinary deck of 52 cards. What is the probability of Gambit drawing 2 Kings (without replacement)?

A. 0

B. $\dfrac{1}{169}$

C. $\dfrac{1}{221}$

D. $\dfrac{4}{663}$

E. None of the above

Question 16:

I have two identical unfair dice, where the probability that the dice get a 6 is twice as high as the probability of any other outcome, which are all equally likely. What is the probability that when I roll both dice the total will be 12?

A. 0

B. $\dfrac{4}{49}$

C. $\dfrac{1}{9}$

D. $\dfrac{2}{7}$

E. None of the above

Question 17:
A roulette wheel consists of 36 numbered spots and 1 zero spot (i.e. 37 spots in total). What is the probability that the ball will stop in a spot either divisible by 3 or 2?

A. 0   B. $\frac{25}{37}$ C. $\frac{25}{36}$ D. $\frac{18}{37}$ E. $\frac{24}{37}$

Question 18:
I have a fair coin that I flip 4 times. What is the probability I get 2 heads and 2 tails?

A. $\frac{1}{16}$ C. $\frac{3}{8}$ E. None of the above

B. $\frac{3}{16}$ D. $\frac{9}{16}$

Question 19:
Shivun rolls two fair dice. What is the probability that he gets a total of 5, 6 or 7?

A. $\frac{9}{36}$ C. $\frac{1}{6}$ E. None of the above

B. $\frac{7}{12}$ D. $\frac{5}{12}$

Question 20:
Dr Savary has a bag that contains x red balls, y blue balls and z green balls (and no others). He pulls out a ball, replaces it, and then pulls out another. What is the probability that he picks one red ball and one green ball?

A. $\frac{2(x+y)}{x+y+z}$ C. $\frac{2xz}{(x+y+z)^2}$ E. $\frac{4xz}{(x+y+z)^4}$

B. $\frac{xz}{(x+y+z)^2}$ D. $\frac{(x+z)}{(x+y+z)^2}$ F. More information necessary

Question 21:

Mr Kilbane has a bag that contains x red balls, y blue balls and z green balls (and no others). He pulls out a ball, does **NOT** replace it, and then pulls out another. What is the probability that he picks one red ball and one blue ball?

A. $\dfrac{2xy}{(x+y+z)^2}$

B. $\dfrac{2xy}{(x+y+z)(x+y+z-1)}$

C. $\dfrac{2xy}{(x+y+z)^2}$

D. $\dfrac{xy}{(x+y+z)(x+y+z-1)}$

E. $\dfrac{4xy}{(x+y+z-1)^2}$

F. More information needed

Question 22:

There are two tennis players. The first player wins the point with probability p, and the second player wins the point with probability 1-p. The rules of tennis say that the first player to score four points wins the game, unless the score is 4-3. At this point the first player to get two points ahead wins.

What is the probability that the first player wins in exactly 5 rounds?

A. $4p^4(1\text{-}p)$

B. $p^4(1\text{-}p)$

C. $4p(1\text{-}p)$

D. $4p(1\text{-}p)^4$

E. $4p^5(1\text{-}p)$

F. More information needed.

Question 23:

Solve the equation $\dfrac{4x+7}{2} + 9x + 10 = 7$

A. $\dfrac{22}{13}$

B. $-\dfrac{22}{13}$

C. $\dfrac{10}{13}$

D. $-\dfrac{10}{13}$

E. $\dfrac{13}{22}$

F. $-\dfrac{13}{22}$

Question 24:
The volume of a sphere is $V = \frac{4}{3}\pi r^3$, and the surface area of a sphere is $S = 4\pi r^2$. Express S in terms of V

A. $S = (4\pi)^{2/3}(3V)^{2/3}$

D. $S = (4\pi)^{1/3}(3V)^{2/3}$

B. $S = (8\pi)^{1/3}(3V)^{2/3}$

E. $S = (16\pi)^{1/3}(9V)^{2/3}$

C. $S = (4\pi)^{1/3}(9V)^{2/3}$

Question 25:
Express the volume of a cube, V, in terms of its surface area, S.

A. $V = (S/6)^{3/2}$

C. $V = (6/S)^{3/2}$

E. $V = (S/36)^{1/2}$

B. $V = S^{3/2}$

D. $V = (S/6)^{1/2}$

F. $V = (S/36)^{3/2}$

Question 26:
Solve the equations $4x + 3y = 7$ and $2x + 8y = 12$

A. $(x,y) = \left(\frac{17}{13}, \frac{10}{13}\right)$

D. $(x,y) = (2,1)$

E. $(x,y) = (6,3)$

B. $(x,y) = \left(\frac{10}{13}, \frac{17}{13}\right)$

F. $(x,y) = (3,6)$

C. $(x,y) = (1,2)$

G. No solutions possible.

Question 27:
Rearrange $\frac{(7x+10)}{(9x+5)} = 3y^2 + 2$, to make x the subject.

A. $\dfrac{15\,y^2}{7 - 9(3y^2+2)}$

C. $-\dfrac{15\,y^2}{7 - 9(3y^2+2)}$

E. $-\dfrac{5\,y^2}{7 + 9(3y^2+2)}$

B. $\dfrac{15\,y^2}{7 + 9(3y^2+2)}$

D. $-\dfrac{15\,y^2}{7 + 9(3y^2+2)}$

F. $\dfrac{5\,y^2}{7 + 9(3y^2+2)}$

Question 28:

Simplify $3x \left(\dfrac{3x^7}{x^{\frac{1}{3}}} \right)^3$

A. $9x^{20}$

B. $27x^{20}$

C. $87x^{20}$

D. $9x^{21}$

E. $27x^{21}$

F. $81x^{21}$

Question 29:

Simplify $2x[(2x)^7]^{\frac{1}{14}}$

A. $2x\sqrt{2}\,x^4$

B. $2x\sqrt{2x^3}$

C. $2\sqrt{2}\,x^4$

D. $2\sqrt{2x^3}$

E. $8x^3$

F. $8x$

Question 30:

What is the circumference of a circle with an area of 10π?

A. $2\pi\sqrt{10}$

B. $\pi\sqrt{10}$

C. 10π

D. 20π

E. $\sqrt{10}$

F. More information needed.

Question 31:

If $a.b = (ab) + (a+b)$, then calculate the value of $(3.4).5$

A. 19   B. 54   C. 100   D. 119   E. 132

Question 32:

If $a.b = \dfrac{a^b}{a}$, calculate $(2.3).2$

A. $\dfrac{16}{3}$ B. 1   C. 2   D. 4   E. 8

Question 33:

Solve $x^2 + 3x - 5 = 0$

A. $x = -\dfrac{3}{2} \pm \dfrac{\sqrt{11}}{2}$

B. $x = \dfrac{3}{2} \pm \dfrac{\sqrt{11}}{2}$

C. $x = -\dfrac{3}{2} \pm \dfrac{\sqrt{11}}{4}$

D. $x = \dfrac{3}{2} \pm \dfrac{\sqrt{11}}{4}$

E. $x = \dfrac{3}{2} \pm \dfrac{\sqrt{29}}{2}$

F. $x = -\dfrac{3}{2} \pm \dfrac{\sqrt{29}}{2}$

Question 34:

How many times do the curves $y = x^3$ and $y = x^2 + 4x + 14$ intersect?

A. 0   B. 1   C. 2   D. 3   E. 4

Question 35:

Which of the following graphs **do not** intersect?

1. $y = x$
2. $y = x^2$
3. $y = 1 - x^2$
4. $y = 2$

A. 1 and 2   C. 3 and 4   E. 1 and 4

B. 2 and 3   D. 1 and 3   F. 2 and 4

Question 36:

Calculate the product of 897,653 and 0.009764.

A. 87646.8   C. 876.468   E. 8.76468

B. 8764.68   D. 87.6468   F. 0.876468

Question 37:

Solve for x: $\dfrac{7x+3}{10} + \dfrac{3x+1}{7} = 14$

A. $\dfrac{929}{51}$ B. $\dfrac{949}{47}$ C. $\dfrac{949}{79}$ D. $\dfrac{980}{79}$

Question 38:

What is the area of an equilateral triangle with side length x.

A. $\dfrac{x^2\sqrt{3}}{4}$

B. $\dfrac{x\sqrt{3}}{4}$

C. $\dfrac{x^2}{2}$

D. $\dfrac{x}{2}$

E. x^2

F. x

Question 39:

Simplify $3 - \dfrac{7x(25x^2 - 1)}{49x^2(5x+1)}$

A. $3 - \dfrac{5x-1}{7x}$

B. $3 - \dfrac{5x+1}{7x}$

C. $3 + \dfrac{5x-1}{7x}$

D. $3 + \dfrac{5x+1}{7x}$

E. $3 - \dfrac{5x^2}{49}$

F. $3 + \dfrac{5x^2}{49}$

Question 40:

Solve the equation $x^2 - 10x - 100 = 0$

A. $-5 \pm 5\sqrt{5}$

B. $-5 \pm \sqrt{5}$

C. $5 \pm 5\sqrt{5}$

D. $5 \pm \sqrt{5}$

E. $5 \pm 5\sqrt{125}$

F. $-5 \pm \sqrt{125}$

Question 41:

Rearrange $x^2 - 4x + 7 = y^3 + 2$ to make x the subject.

A. $x = 2 \pm \sqrt{y^3 + 1}$

B. $x = 2 \pm \sqrt{y^3 - 1}$

C. $x = -2 \pm \sqrt{y^3 - 1}$

D. $x = -2 \pm \sqrt{y^3 + 1}$

E. x cannot be made the subject for this equation.

Question 42:

Rearrange $3x + 2 = \sqrt{7x^2 + 2x + y}$ to make y the subject.

A. $y = 4x^2 + 8x + 2$

B. $y = 4x^2 + 8x + 4$

C. $y = 2x^2 + 10x + 2$

D. $y = 2x^2 + 10x + 4$

E. $y = x^2 + 10x + 2$

F. $y = x^2 + 10x + 4$

Question 43:

Rearrange $y^4 - 4y^3 + 6y^2 - 4y + 2 = x^5 + 7$ to make y the subject.

A. $y = 1 + (x^5 + 7)^{1/4}$

B. $y = -1 + (x^5 + 7)^{1/4}$

C. $y = 1 + (x^5 + 6)^{1/4}$

D. $y = -1 + (x^5 + 6)^{1/4}$

Question 44:

The aspect ratio of my television screen is 4:3 and the diagonal is 50 inches. What is the area of my television screen?

A. 1,200 inches²

B. 1,000 inches²

C. 120 inches²

D. 100 inches²

E. More information needed.

Question 45:

Rearrange the equation $\sqrt{1 + 3x^{-2}} = y^5 + 1$ to make x the subject.

A. $x = \frac{(y^{10} + 2y^5)}{3}$

B. $x = \frac{3}{(y^{10} + 2y^5)}$

C. $x = \sqrt{\frac{3}{y^{10} + 2y^5}}$

D. $x = \sqrt{\frac{y^{10} + 2y^5}{3}}$

E. $x = \sqrt{\frac{y^{10} + 2y^5 + 2}{3}}$

F. $x = \sqrt{\frac{3}{y^{10} + 2y^5 + 2}}$

Question 46:

Solve $3x - 5y = 10$ and $2x + 2y = 13$.

A. $(x, y) = (\frac{19}{16}, \frac{85}{16})$

B. $(x, y) = (\frac{85}{16}, -\frac{19}{16})$

C. $(x, y) = (\frac{85}{16}, \frac{19}{16})$

D. $(x, y) = (-\frac{85}{16}, -\frac{19}{16})$

E. No solutions possible.

Question 47:

The two inequalities $x + y \leq 3$ and $x^3 - y^2 < 3$ define a region on a plane. Which of the following points is inside the region?

A. (2, 1)   C. (1, 2)   E. (1, 2.5)

B. (2.5, 1)   D. (3, 5)   F. None of the above.

Question 48:

How many times do $y = x + 4$ and $y = 4x^2 + 5x + 5$ intersect?

A. 0   B. 1   C. 2   D. 3   E. 4

Question 49:

How many times do $y = x^3$ and $y = x$ intersect?

A. 0   B. 1   C. 2   D. 3   E. 4

Question 50:

A cube has unit length sides. What is the length of a line joining a vertex to the midpoint of the opposite side?

A. $\sqrt{2}$

B. $\sqrt{\frac{3}{2}}$

C. $\sqrt{3}$

D. $\sqrt{5}$

E. $\frac{\sqrt{5}}{2}$

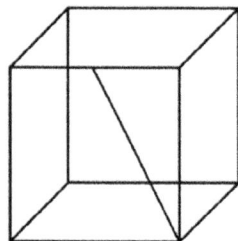

Question 51:

Solve for x, y, and z.

1. $x + y - z = -1$
2. $2x - 2y + 3z = 8$
3. $2x - y + 2z = 9$

	x	y	z
A	2	-15	-14
B	15	2	14
C	14	15	-2
D	-2	15	14
E	2	-15	14
F	No solutions possible		

Question 52:

Fully factorise: $3a^3 - 30a^2 + 75a$

A. $3a(a - 3)^3$ C. $3a(a^2 - 10a + 25)$ E. $3a(a + 5)$

B. $a(3a - 5)^2$ D. $3a(a - 5)^2$

Question 53:

Solve for x and y:

$$4x + 3y = 48$$
$$3x + 2y = 34$$

	x	y
A	8	6
B	6	8
C	3	4
D	4	3
E	30	12
F	12	30
G	No solutions possible	

Question 54:

Evaluate: $\dfrac{-\left(5^2-4\times 7\right)^2}{-6^2+2\times 7}$

A. $-\dfrac{3}{50}$

B. $\dfrac{11}{22}$

C. $-\dfrac{3}{22}$

D. $\dfrac{9}{50}$

E. $\dfrac{9}{22}$

F. 0

Question 55:

All license plates are 6 characters long. The first 3 characters consist of letters and the next 3 characters of numbers. How many unique license plates are possible?

A. 676,000

B. 6,760,000

C. 67,600,000

D. 1,757,600

E. 17,576,000

F. 175,760,000

Question 56:

How many solutions are there for: $2(2(x^2-3x)) = -9$

A. 0

B. 1

C. 2

D. 3

E. Infinite solutions.

Question 57:

Evaluate: $\left(x^{\frac{1}{2}}\,y^{-3}\right)^{\frac{1}{2}}$

A. $\dfrac{x^{\frac{1}{2}}}{y}$

B. $\dfrac{x}{y^{\frac{3}{2}}}$

C. $\dfrac{x^{\frac{1}{4}}}{y^{\frac{3}{2}}}$

D. $\dfrac{y^{\frac{1}{4}}}{x^{\frac{3}{2}}}$

Question 58:

Bryan earned a total of £ 1,240 last week from renting out three flats. From this, he had to pay 10% of the rent from the 1-bedroom flat for repairs, 20% of the rent from the 2-bedroom flat for repairs, and 30% from the 3-bedroom flat for repairs. The 3-bedroom flat costs twice as much as the 1-bedroom flat. Given that the total repair bill was £ 276 calculate the rent for each apartment.

	1 Bedroom	2 Bedrooms	3 Bedrooms
A	280	400	560
B	140	200	280
C	420	600	840
D	250	300	500
E	500	600	1,000

Question 59:

Evaluate: $5 [5(6^2 - 5 \times 3) + 400^{\frac{1}{2}}]^{1/3} + 7$

A. 0
B. 25

C. 32
D. 49

E. 56
F. 200

Question 60:

What is the area of a regular hexagon with side length 1?

A. $3\sqrt{3}$

B. $\frac{3\sqrt{3}}{2}$

C. $\sqrt{3}$

D. $\frac{\sqrt{3}}{2}$

E. 6

F. More information needed

Question 61:

Dexter moves into a new rectangular room that is 19 metres longer than it is wide, and its total area is 780 square metres. What are the room's dimensions?

A. Width = 20 m; Length = -39 m
B. Width = 20 m; Length = 39 m
C. Width = 39 m; Length = 20 m
D. Width = -39 m; Length = 20 m
E. Width = -20 m; Length = 39 m

Question 62:

Tom uses 34 meters of fencing to enclose his rectangular lot. He measured the diagonals to 13 metres long. What is the length and width of the lot?

A. 3 m by 4 m   C. 6 m by 12 m   E. 9 m by 15 m
B. 5 m by 12 m   D. 8 m by 15 m   F. 10 m by 10 m

Question 63:

Solve $\dfrac{3x-5}{2} + \dfrac{x+5}{4} = x + 1$

A. 1   C. 3   E. 4.5
B. 1.5   D. 3.5   F. None of the above

Question 64:

Calculate: $\dfrac{5.226 \times 10^6 + 5.226 \times 10^5}{1.742 \times 10^{10}}$

A. 0.033   C. 0.00033   E. 0.0000033
B. 0.0033   D. 0.000033

Question 65:

Calculate the area of the triangle shown to the right:

A. $3 + \sqrt{2}$ D. $3 - \sqrt{2}$

B. $\dfrac{2 + 2\sqrt{2}}{2}$ E. 3

C. $2 + 5\sqrt{2}$ F. 6

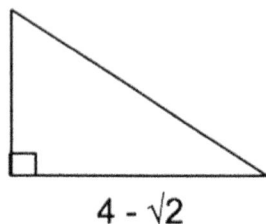

$2 + \sqrt{2}$

$4 - \sqrt{2}$

Question 66:

Rearrange $\sqrt{\dfrac{4}{x}} + 9 = y - 2$ to make x the subject.

A. $x = \dfrac{11}{(y-2)^2}$ C. $x = \dfrac{4}{(y+1)(y-5)}$ E. $x = \dfrac{4}{(y+1)(y+5)}$

B. $x = \dfrac{9}{(y-2)^2}$ D. $x = \dfrac{4}{(y-1)(y+5)}$ F. $x = \dfrac{4}{(y-1)(y-5)}$

Question 67:
When 5 is subtracted from 5x the result is half the sum of 2 and 6x. What is the value of x?

A. 0   B. 1   C. 2   D. 3   E. 4   F. 6

Question 68:
Estimate $\dfrac{54.98 + 2.25^2}{\sqrt{905}}$

A. 0   B. 1   C. 2   D. 3   E. 4   F. 5

Question 69:
At a Pizza Parlour, you can order single, double or triple cheese in the crust. You also have the option to include ham, olives, pepperoni, bell pepper, meat balls, tomato slices, and pineapples. How many different types of pizza are available at the Pizza Parlour?

A. 10   C. 192   E. 768
B. 96   D. 384   F. None of the above

Question 70:
Solve the simultaneous equations $x^2 + y^2 = 1$ and $x + y = \sqrt{2}$, for x, y > 0

A. $(x, y) = (\frac{\sqrt{2}}{2}, \frac{\sqrt{2}}{2})$ C. $(x, y) = (\sqrt{2} - 1, 1)$

B. $(x, y) = (\frac{1}{2}, \frac{\sqrt{3}}{2})$ D. $(x, y) = (\sqrt{2}, \frac{1}{2})$

Question 71:
Which of the following statements is **FALSE**?

A. Congruent objects always have the same dimensions and shape.
B. Congruent objects can be mirror images of each other.
C. Congruent objects do not always have the same angles.
D. Congruent objects can be rotations of each other.
E. Two triangles are congruent if they have two sides and one angle of the same magnitude.

Question 72:
Solve the inequality $x^2 \geq 6 - x$

A. $x \leq -3$ and $x \leq 2$

B. $x \leq -3$ and $x \geq 2$

C. $x \geq -3$ and $x \leq 2$

D. $x \geq -3$ and $x \geq 2$

E. $x \geq 2$ only

F. $x \geq -3$ only

Question 73:
The hypotenuse of an isosceles right-angled triangle is x cm. What is the area of the triangle in terms of x?

A. $\frac{\sqrt{x}}{2}$

B. $\frac{x^2}{4}$

C. $\frac{x}{4}$

D. $\frac{3x^2}{4}$

E. $\frac{x^2}{10}$

Question 74:
Mr Heard derives a formula: $Q = \frac{(X+Y)^2 A}{3B}$. He doubles the values of X and Y, halves the value of A and triples the value of B. What happens to value of Q?

A. Decreases by $\frac{1}{3}$

B. Increases by $\frac{1}{3}$

C. Decreases by $\frac{2}{3}$

D. Increases by $\frac{2}{3}$

E. Increases by $\frac{4}{3}$

F. Decreases by $\frac{4}{3}$

Question 75:
Consider the graphs $y = x^2 - 2x + 3$, and $y = x^2 - 6x - 10$. Which of the following is true?

A. Both equations intersect the x-axis.

B. Neither equation intersects the x-axis.

C. The first equation does not intersect the x-axis; the second equation intersects the x-axis.

D. The first equation intersects the x-axis; the second equation does not intersect the x-axis.

ANSWERS

ACADEMIC LITERACY: ANSWER KEY

Q	A	Q	A	Q	A	Q	A	Q	A
1	B	21	B	41	A	61	A	81	A
2	C	22	C	42	C	62	C	82	C
3	B	23	C	43	C	63	D	83	D
4	B	24	D	44	B	64	C	84	A
5	D	25	C	45	B	65	C	85	A
6	C	26	D	46	A	66	A	86	C
7	B	27	B	47	A	67	B	87	D
8	D	28	C	48	C	68	A	88	A
9	C	29	C	49	C	69	A	89	C
10	D	30	C	50	B	70	C	90	A
11	A	31	B	51	A	71	B	91	B
12	C	32	B	52	D	72	C	92	C
13	C	33	D	53	B	73	B	93	C
14	A	34	A	54	A	74	D	94	B
15	C	35	B	55	C	75	C	95	D
16	C	36	C	56	C	76	C	96	D
17	D	37	C	57	B	77	B	97	C
18	B	38	C	58	B	78	A	98	B
19	A	39	C	59	A	79	B	99	A
20	D	40	C	60	D	80	C		

ACADEMIC LITERACY: WORKED ANSWERS

Set 1:
1. **B-** The passage suggests that the critics suppose 'human beings to be capable of no pleasures except those of which swine are capable', and so suggest the potential of higher pleasures. They do not call their critics degraded, but suggest that the critics degrade human nature, nor do they accuse critics of being either miserable or indulgent.
2. **C-** This action does not see happiness as its justification, but conforming to social norms. It does not seek to increase pleasure or reduce pain, just follow dogma, which is not according to the principle of utility.
3. **B-** Mill does not describe the religious views of his critics, or explicitly call them reactionary, and in fact describes them 'some of the most estimable in feeling and purpose'. He does mention the countries of origin for some of his critics, and they are all in Europe.
4. **B-** The passage also states 'desirable things' could be 'means' to pleasure.
5. **D-**Utility is defined as the foundation of the system, and a belief that the increasing of happiness/decreasing of happiness is good. The passage specifically states that it has not given an exhaustive definition of things that are pleasurable/painful, and it does not specifically define Epicureans, simply suggests a link between them and utilitarian's - which is not an exhaustive explanation of the term.

Set 2:
6. **C-**Though sandstone is made from sand, the passage does not state that ALL rocks are made from this material.
7. **B-**The passage discusses the valley when implementing the wall-building analogy.
8. **D-** 'Some ancient source' is all we are told, and so the source is undisclosed (Paragraph 3).
9. **C-** This rock is said in paragraph 2 to be found 'everywhere', so not 'nowhere'.
10. **D-** Paragraph 3: The grains are said to be sorted in groups 'of a size', i.e. measurements. They are all described as 'worn and rounded', and no mention is made of differentiation through age/shape.

Set 3:

11. **A-** Though the flowers smell pleasant, no mention is made of this scent being used to manufacture perfumes.

12. **C-** The passage states that the flower could bloom more than once a century, precluding 'D', but that it is thought to only do so in a century, providing evidence for 'C'.

13. **C-** The statement claims that Narcissus plants are 'prized by many' over Lilies, but this does not mean that all people - or even the majority of people - think the former is more attractive/better than the latter, or that all homeowners enjoy the plant.

14. **A-** It is actually a substance 'very similar to rum', not rum itself.

15. **C-** The genus 'belongs' to the family, as stated in paragraph 1.

Set 4:

16. **C-**Women in Illinois, not across USA, were subject to the law, and the passage does not state either a change in fashion or actual arrests, only the potential for arrests.

17. **D-** The pulling out of feathers from live birds was seen as the negative to using osprey feathers.

18. **B-** They could be possessed only 'in their proper season'.

19. **A-** The problem cited is that the article was already in use in the clothing of numerous military men. The authority of the princess/sexist politics does not feature in the passage, and 'D' is patently false

20. **D-** None of those are precluded, as only 'harmless' and 'dead' birds (in their entirety) were prohibited. Wearing a living bird was not explicitly banned.

Set 5:

21. **B-** Nothing in the above passage provides evidence for 'C', 'D' or 'A' - in fact, the 'indie' description of Pope opposes the idea of him working for a games company at all. 'B' is supported by the fact the game is available on a number of devices and system operators.

22. **C-** The immigration officer's job is to process people correctly - not to grow or limit the number of immigrants, as in 'A' and 'B'. 'D' is vague, as 'to stamp passports' does not necessarily mean to stamp them correctly, and false stamps would be counter to the purpose of the border guard's position.

23. **C-** Though the game player may perform either a body scan or finger print check when something is amiss is the candidate's documents, they will not necessarily do either of these - first, they will 'enquire', which is synonymous with 'C', 'asking…for further information'. The only one of the statements that will be universally true for discrepancies therefore is c.

24. **D-** The game-player may accept 'bribes', so 'A' is not true. The game player 'may' arrest candidates, but the passage does not state he or she must, so 'B' is false. The game-player is allowed two mistakes, so to an extent, can be forgiven - making 'C' incorrect. As further mistakes will lead to being 'pecuniarily punished', 'D' is the only accurate statement.

Set 6:

25. **C-** The head of LA NAACP is a civil rights' activist.

26. **D-** The other aspects may appear in films, but only racial slurs were cited as a 'common' element without specifying location of setting of sub-type.

27. **B-** 'Primarily' means the same as 'predominately' in this case, and the cast has been described as 'predominately' black - meaning most, but not all, cast members are black.

28. **C-** Original intended audiences were black city-dwellers: 'B' is too broad and 'A' is too narrow. 'D' is not at all supported in the passage. 'C' describes the growing audience, and how the genre is now 'not exclusive to any race' (Paragraph 2)

29. **C-** It is possible, but nothing in the statement suggests the potentially racy titles are a nod towards sexploitation genre. The innuendo may be incidental, or the choice of words completely divorced from the pornographic films of the past.

Set 7:

30. **C-** It would be a massive assumption to state that just because two characters in a book are 'vicious', all of them will be, so 'A' is not necessarily correct. 'B' also believes in a despair that is described to belong to the Comedian, but not Rorscach. The argument of the passage is that 'D', which Moore may believe, is not the case - the beloved character is not simply worshipped for his violence, but for his belief in justice. 'C' is correct, as Moore describes how he wished Rorschach not to be a favourite character, but a warning.

31. **B-** False. The fact he finds things a 'joke' is what makes him the Comedian. He may not be all that funny, but the joke is still there.

32. **B-** He does not mention madness ('D'), or invoke shame ('C'), or simply state it is good to be good ('A') - specifically, he states we must act as if the world is 'just', even when not, to attain dignity.

33. **D-** No value judgment is made comparing violent actions or on the Comedian's jokes so 'A' and 'B' are false. The passage also acknowledge Rorschach's violence, showing 'C' is wrong, but does state that his actions are due to the fact he believes he is acting in the name of justice, which lends him an ethical justification to his actions.

34. **A-** The lack of meaning in anything is what leads him to treat everything as a joke - it is not hatred, but the inability to see 'purpose' in himself or his fellow man.

Set 8:

35. **B-** The passage's explanation of The Bechdel Test does not state that the test is used to show 'sexism', so a failed film does not equate to a sexist one.

36. **C-** This is the only film that shows a female-female conversation not on a man. 'A' and 'B' only feature conversations focused on males and 'D' does not have two women speaking to one another.

37. **C-** Though of the two horror films mentioned in the extract one passes it and another one fails, the passage does not make use this to make any claims on the genre as a whole.

38. **C-** Her comment that it is 'strict' shows she has a reservation, but her general agreeing that it is a 'good idea' shows she approves of the notion. Her statement is too qualified to be described by 'A', too positive to be understood by 'B', and contains a judgement precluding 'C' as a correct statement.

39. **C-** The two women are not named within the comic strip - though two women are behind the idea (one in suggesting it, the other in illustrating it), that is not to say that the two depicted women are the same.

Set 9:

40. **C-** The possible 'idea' that repetition is funny is inherently funny is mentioned, but neither confirmed nor denied.

41. **A-** This is the only statement actually mentioned above. Laughing twice at the same joke does not make it 'twice as funny', that is a logical fallacy; it does not state that all relationships dictate that the two parties find themselves funny (this is too vague) and being 'comfortable' is not cited as encouraging laughter.

42. **C-** There is no mention of a humour requirement for the first joke.

43. **C-** Though the call-back here is described as a comic trope, this does not necessarily preclude the same device being used in something un-comic: in the same way word-play or alliteration can be used to achieve a multitude effects, not all humorous.

44. **B-** Though 'A' is a potential, it is not a requirement of the call back, and 'C' is not supported through the passage's material. At no point is the call-back named significant, compared to other tropes: it is simply one that the passage focuses on. It does however state that it can be used by a comedian, and used for comedy, so 'B' is correct.

Set 10:

45. **B-** She was the fourth, after Catherine, Mary and her namesake Harriet Elizabeth, who died as an infant.

46. **A-** He was a 'Rev', a reverend, and a 'divine'. She was born in the USA, not UK, and in the 19th century. Her town is said to be 'characteristic', and so not 'average'.

47. **A-** She is said to have 'veneration' in all who knew her.

48. **C-** It is only described as the 'most sad' and 'most tender' memory of her childhood, not her life. It is, however, described as 'the first memorable incident' and thus the earliest one of her life.

49. **C-** She wrote her Charles, so at least wrote one letter. The autobiography mentioned belonged to her brother, not her, and she had five brothers and sisters waiting for her when she was born, not only brothers. She was actually four when her mother died, as the narrator tells us, and her remembering being between 'three and four' is a false memory.

Set 11:

50. **B-** He thought it was 'a pity that only rich people could own books', and from this he 'finally determined to contrive' of a new way of printing. The passage does not state that he wished to make money, found books too expensive to get a hold of or was impatient himself when it came to the production of books.

51. **A-** The need to be careful is mentioned, as is the fact that the process takes a long time both in creating the block and due to the fact one block can only print one page. That it may tire a carver to make the block is possible, but it is not cited in the passage.

52. **D-** The statement says it is 'very likely' he was taught to read, but is not definite. That his father comes from a 'good family' does not mean he is a member of the aristocracy, necessarily. Though block printing was used as the boy grew up, it does not state this was the most popular process. The mention of Gutenberg's family's 'wealthy friends' indicates they were sociable.

53. **B-** The paper was laid on top of the block, not underneath.

54. **A-** There is nothing written in the passage praising the craftsmanship of manuscripts. The appropriateness of the titles for both book production processes is explained, and the 'wealthy friends' are described as a source to borrow books from, thus a way of expanding your reading.

Set 12:

55. **C-** In both examples given above, Apollo is the giver - but these are only two of 'several' versions, and it is possible others exist.

56. **C-** The gift of prophecy is supernatural, therefore this is the best answer. There is no evidence to suggest that she knew chastity would lead to her tragic fate, that she is 'often' seen as a home wrecker (though she is killed by Clytemnestra, this does not prove Cassandra, the slave, is perceived as a vindictive 'other woman') or that parents use the name to express hate – they may just like the sound, and not care about its history, or not know the history at all.

57. **B-** Nothing is said about the state of Cassandra's childhood, but it is mentioned that plays are written about her and that Homer has written about her, showing 'C' and 'D' are true. The fact her father was a king proves she was from a royal line.

58. **B-** The passage states the 'presentation of her character alters'.
59. **A-** It is not said that she ignores or refuses to accept the gift, or demands more presents, even in the first story, just that she refuses to sleep with him. Only the broken promise, as described in the second version of the myth, is mentioned above.

Set 13:

60. **D-** The passage attacks a generalisation, and shows an example that refutes one given to the 'musical' genre. Nothing is mentioned of Sondheim's talents, or what his role was in creating the musical, nor are their claims made to Wheeler's literary tastes (he may just like ONE penny dreadful). This musical may deal with morbid themes, but that's not to say that most do - it could be only a select few that do.
61. **A-** The pies make the crimes 'culinary' in nature, the mention of revenge shows Todd's illegal acts to be 'vengeful' and the judge's rape is a 'sexual' crime. There is nothing explicitly suggesting the crimes of any party are funny, or to be considered funny.
62. **C-** Though the original title 'A String of Pearls: A Romance' may appear to suggest a romantic relationship within the narrative, nothing in the passage states the two are a couple.
63. **D-** Is essentially synonymous is the quoted belief, 'we all deserve to die', which include both bad and good people and makes no significant reference to gender exclusion/inclusion.
64. C- There are four mentioned themes, but that does not mean there are only four themes, nor does 'legal corruption' get named as the central theme. As the entirety of Sweeney Todd is not discussed in the passage, only a central plot line, one could not exclude the potential of something positive happening in the play - even a minor incident. The themes mentioned are, however, indeed macabre.

Set 14:

65. **C-** The above passage is about WWII trains, not WWI ones.
66. **A-** The soldier makes a chair by using a tipped-up suitcase. It is a marine, not a sailor, learning on the back of a chair, and the passage states 'some', not 'many' queue for two hours to go to the diner car, whilst similarly 'some' (not necessarily 'many') go hungry.

67. **B-** The passage discourages mothers from going on trains with a baby, stating they should only do it as a necessity.

68. **A-** 'At every stop' more people come on the train.

69. **A-** The passage does not insult anyone, but it does say the railroads are doing their job 'well'.

Set 15:

70. **C** The passage states the slice of bread is an ounce, and contains 3/4 ounce of flour, making it 75% flour.

71. **B-** It says it is possible that they do, but also possible that they don't. There is no emphatic claim.

72. **C-** It is over a million loaves a day, 319 million pounds - not bushels - a year and 365,000 loaves - not over - a year.

73. **B-** False. It may seem unimportant, but the passage goes on to explain how a single slice of bread has value.

74. **D-** The government have researched waste, but not taken responsibility for it, nor is it said they should do more to combat this. The final sentence confirms that housekeepers are responsible for their own food wastage.

Set 16:

75. **C-** Fourteen women and three men are described to be arrested.

76. **C-** She was the only woman, but it does not state whether either man was brought to trial.

77. **B-** The majority ultimately rule, but Hall 'dissented', or disagreed, with the other two originally.

78. **A-** It is said that it was proved upon trial that she was informed of a right to vote and had no doubt over her entitlement at the time of voting.

79. **B-** They were charged independently.

Set 17:

80. **C-** Nowhere does it state that all European countries have similar creatures (though certain types can be found in both British Isles and Norway) nor does it state the array of animals is limited to this one nation. Sharing animals and birds does not necessitate sharing geographical features, but it is said a country with forest and moorlands is likely to have a variety of birds and animals, so one can see the link between forests and creatures.

81. **A-** There was a time when the English dreaded wolves and bears, but that indicates the past, or at least does not include the present. Norwegians being superior is not suggested here.

82. **C-** Bears are called destroyers, which is sufficient to conclude they cause damage.

83. **D-** They are ruthlessly hunted by farmers in country districts, but numerous only in the forest tracts in the Far North.

84. **A-** The word fortunately implies that it is good the wolves are no longer central. The children are under no threat, as the threat of wolves belongs to a bygone time, there is no mention of regret that such a time is gone and Norsemen are not demonstrated in the above passage to have respect for Nature, but instead they are said to interfere with it through hunting and driving wolves farther afield from their current homes.

Set 18:

85. **A-** They were seen as the 'friendly or hostile manifestation of some higher powers, demonical and Divine.' The 'manifestation' of the 'Divine' could be interpreted as a religious quality.

86. **C-** A small minority believe that dreams are not the dreamer's own psychical act, meaning the majority believe that they are.

87. **D-** There is incongruity between feelings and images, suggesting a lack of a logical link between the two. Waking thoughts are said to find some dreams repugnant, and though dreams are described as forgotten, that is not necessarily due to them being dull.

88. **A-** It asks can sense be made of each single dream.

89. **C-** A link between the psychical sleeping and waking self is suggested, but not definitively proved. Pre-scientific communities, according to the passage, had a hypothesis that left them with 'no uncertainty'. The 'origin of the dream' remains a question in Freud's writing that has been left without a satisfactory answer. That 'our reminiscences' may 'mutilate' a dream is mentioned, leaving 'C' the only statement with support from the passage.

Set 19:

90. **A**-"Most" requires over half by definition, and "most" of the people living in this area were the descendants of immigrants who moved to the country a "full century ago".

91. **B**- Hall only makes a claim for New England, not the entirety of America, being the descendants of 20,000 immigrants. The 'one million' figure comes from Franklin, not Hall. Less than 80,000 ("under" 80,000) people led to the population boom of one million. One million is over ten times (under) 80,000, so "b" is correct.

92. **C**- It is said to be "distinct" to older aristocracy "of the royal governor's courts". It is not similar to any European aristocracy. There is no specific reference to it not being a system based on lineage.

93. **C**- It says that these were the texts read by the most people, but that does not mean they were the most plentiful – other books may have outnumbered the bibles, even if they received fewer readers.

94. **B**- "A", "c" and "d" are cited in the passage (the journey took 'the better part of the year', it was 'hazardous' and 'expensive'), whereas 'B' is not referenced at all.

Set 20:

95. **D** – Paragraph 2 states that the "main thing" which must be considered when assessing Russia's role is the sapping of the German, Austro-Hungarian and Turkish resources.

96. **5** – America, Italy, Romania and Britain are mentioned at the end of paragraph 1, and France in paragraph 3.

97. **C** – Russia certainly had a greater role when compared to America, Italy, Romania & Britain (paragraph 1). However, there are no details of France's efforts throughout the war.

98. **B** – A & C contributed, but the final catastrophe of the Central Powers was the direct consequence of the offensive of the Allies in 1918 (paragraph 2). Thus, as this was the final catastrophe, this can be concluded to be what won the war.

99. **A** – The final paragraph states that both Russia's and France's efforts were required to stop Germany from the winning the war, which they came very close to.

QUANTITATIVE LITERACY: ANSWER KEY

Q	A	Q	A	Q	A	Q	A	Q	A
1	C	26	B	51	A	76	C	101	A
2	D	27	D	52	E	77	B	102	E
3	D	28	B	53	C	78	D	103	A
4	D	29	B	54	E	79	D	104	C
5	C	30	B	55	C	80	C	105	B
6	B	31	C	56	A	81	B	106	C
7	A	32	C	57	D	82	C	107	C
8	A	33	A	58	D	83	A	108	B
9	B	34	C	59	C	84	C	109	B
10	A	35	B	60	D	85	C	110	C
11	D	36	D	61	C	86	B	111	D
12	B	37	C	62	A	87	C	112	C
13	A	38	B	63	E	88	C	113	E
14	B	39	D	64	E	89	B	114	E
15	B	40	B	65	C	90	D	115	C
16	D	41	C	66	B	91	C		
17	B	42	A	67	B	92	D		
18	D	43	E	68	D	93	C		
19	B	44	A	69	D	94	E		
20	B	45	E	70	D	95	E		
21	B	46	C	71	D	96	B		
22	B	47	A	72	C	97	D		
23	C	48	D	73	D	98	C		
24	B	49	D	74	A	99	D		
25	B	50	C	75	A	100	A		

QUANTITATIVE LITERACY: WORKED ANSWERS

SET 1

Question 1: C

We can work out that the tax rates must fit in the following equation:
($50 x Food tax rate) + ($30 x Clothes tax rate) + $80 = $88. Only the tax rates in Casova fit correctly in this equation.

Question 2: D

To answer this question, we calculate how much the supplier will make for selling the items, by considering the tax rate in each state, and deducting it from the price accordingly.

Thus, in Bolovia, each year the supplier makes 250 x ($40/1.20 + $40/1.15 + $40/1.10 + $40/1.15) = $34,812 a year. In Asteria, each year the supplier makes 250 x ($40/1.10 + $40/1.15 + $40/1.10 + $40/1.15) = $35,572. (Note that in the case of an item being applicable to 2 tax rates, the higher rate will be charged. Thus, in Bolovia, imported clothes will be charged at the clothes tax rate of 15%, since this is higher than the imports rate.)

Thus, by moving to Asteria, the supplier will make $760 more each year. Therefore it will take 26.3 years to recover the purchase cost of $20,000.

Question 3: D

If John spends $88, he will spend £12 on tax. Thus, the tax rate is 12/88 = 13.6%. If John shops in Asteria, the maximum tax rate he would have to pay is 10%; at Casova it would be 10%. If he spends at least $50 on food in Derivia, he pays no tax on it. Thus, he can spend a maximum of $38 on imported goods (at a maximum tax rate of 15%). This equates to a tax of $5.70 (not $12). Finally, if John spends $10 on imported goods in Bolovia – he would pay $0.50 in tax. Thus, he can spend up to $78 on clothes taxed at 15%. The tax on the clothes is therefore $11.70, giving $12.20 tax in total as the maximum. Since he pays $12 dollars tax, he shops in Bolovia.

Question 4: D

The sum of the basic prices is 100+30+10+100 = $240. Now the highest tax rate on the board is 20% (for imports to Asteria), thus the maximum tax is $240 x 1.20 = $288. However, this is impossible to attain (since if we bought everything in Asteria, the ham would be cheaper, as it is not imported and would only be taxed at the food rate). Therefore no option allows the overall price to be as high as $288, so this is the answer. Answer A) is possible if all products were bought in the state they are produced in. Answer C) is the correct answer if all products were bought in Asteria (and accounting for the reduced tax rate for the ham, which is not an import). Answer B) is possible if the ham was bought in Asteria, the caviar and orange juice were bought in Casova and the dress was bought in Bolovia.

SET 2

Question 5: C

Firstly, find the pressure it can withstand in Pascals: 200 pounds per square inch x 7,000 Pascals per pound per square inch = 1.4 million Pascals.

Then divide this by 1,000 Pa to get the depth the probe can withstand (we can see from the question that the pressure increases by 1,000 Pa for every metre depth increase):

1,400,000/1,000 = 1,400 metres into the ocean, which is 1.4 km.

Question 6: B

Calculate that the probe can drop 300,000 Pa/1,000 Pa per metre = 300 metres into the ocean before breaking.

Now rearrange the equation in the question, to make t the subject, as follows:

$2d = \sqrt{(t^3)}$

$(2d)^2 = t^3$

$t = \sqrt[3]{(2d)^2}$

Then substitute the depth into this supplied equation:

$t = \sqrt[3]{(2d)^2} = \sqrt[3]{(2 \times 300)^2} = 71$ seconds.

SET 3

Question 7: A

Calculate the amount of drug taken for each disease:

Black Trump Virus = 4 mg x 80 kg x 3 times a day x 28 days = 26.88 g

Swamp Fever = 3x80x1x7 = 1.68 g

Yellow Tick = 1x80x2x84 = 13.44 g

Red Rage = 5x80x2x21 = 16.80 g

At a quick glance, the swamp fever dosage is much lower than all the others – you can discount this and use that to save a little time if you need to.

Question 8: A

First calculate that Carol took 20.16 grams of the drug during the two courses for Yellow Tick, using the same method as for John, but using Carol's weight of 60kg. Therefore 20.16 grams (the amount left over) corresponds to the dosage for the unknown disease:

4x60x3x28 = 20.16 g, therefore the unknown disease was Black Trump Virus.

Question 9: B

The first time he takes $3 \times 80 \times 1 \times 7 = 1.68$ grams, and the second time he takes $4 \times 110 \times 3 \times 28 = 36.96$ grams. Thus the ratio is 1.68 : 36.96 = 1:22.

Question 10: A

By calculating the dose required in each of the cases, we see that the only one that is above 15.5 grams over 4 weeks is the dosage for Red Rage:

$5 \times 75 \times 2 \times 21 = 15.75$ g – therefore Danny must be suffering from Red Rage.

Question 11: D

Heavier people need a higher dose. To find the maximum weight, we use the equation: $5 \times$ weight $\times 2 \times 21 = 10$ g, where "weight" represents the maximum weight requiring a dosage of less than 10 g.

So the maximum weight to not need a dosage exceeding 10 g is = 10,000 mg/(21 days x 2 daily doses x 5 mg/kg) = 47.62 kg.

SET 4

Question 12: B

To solve this, divide the flour content by the overall mass. A quick inspection might show you that this is likely to be Madeira, which is confirmed by the calculation (250/825 = 0.3). Thus, 30% of the Madeira's total weight is flour, which is a higher percentage than for any other cake

Question 13: A

In this question, there must be one cake where: (2,600/mass of cake) = (625/mass of flour in cake). Thus, there is a number that both the mass of the cake and the mass of flour can be multiplied by, in order to get these numbers respectively.

We can see that if we multiply the mass of the sponge cake by 5, we get 2,600 g. Equally, if we multiply the mass of flour in the sponge cake recipe (125g) by 5, then we get 625 g. Thus, Sponge cake is the answer. No other cake recipe can be multiplied by a given number to get an overall weight of 2,600 g and 625 g of flour.

Question 14: B

We use 1.50+1.25+1.10+1 times the ingredients for one cake, so the wedding cake will use 4.85 times as much of the ingredients listed for one cakes. We can use this to find which of the possible answers can be the amount of sugar in the cake, i.e. the sugar called for in one recipe multiplied by 4.85.

The quickest way to do this is to divide each possible answer by 4.85, and see if the result matches the weight of sugar in any of the cakes. We see that 970 g/4.85 = 200 g, which is the amount of sugar in the chocolate cake. None of the other amounts are possible. Thus, B is the answer.

Question 15: B

A kilogram of flour costs 55 x 2/3 pence and we are using 0.25 kg, so 9.167 p worth of flour goes into a Madeira cake. For sugar, we have 0.175 kg x 70 p per kg = 12.25 p worth of sugar going into the cake.

The ratio is thus 9.167:12.25 = approx 0.75:1 = 3:4

Question 16: D

As before, the flour costs: 55 p per 1.5 kg x 2/3 x 0.2 kg = 7.3 pence.
The milk costs: 44 p per kg x 150 g/1000 g per kg = 6.6 pence.
Thus the ratio is 7.3:6.6 = 1:0.9 = 10:9.

SET 5
Question 17: B
In total, 108 people out of the 200 tested have the disease; this is 108/200 = 0.54. Thus, the answer is 54%.

Question 18: D
As the infection rate is different for men and women, the infection rates must be calculated separately and combined:
(231,768 x 0.53 women x 0.63) + (231,768 x 0.47 men x 0.45) = 126,406 to the nearest whole person.

Question 19: B
There are 45 men and 63 women in the test group who have the Kryptos virus. Thus 15 of the men and 45 of the women have visited Atlantis. As we now know that 60 people have visited Atlantis, we can see that 108 − 60 = 48 have not visited. Now we simply calculate 48 as a percentage of 108. 48/108 = 0.44. Thus, 44% of people testing positive for the Virus in Test A have *not* visited Atlantis.

Question 20: B
We can see that 20/45 men testing positive in Test A have also tested positive in Test B, so we assume that the rest were false positives stemming from the inaccuracies of Test A. We are told to assume the same proportion of false positives in the women tested, so we simply apply this fraction to the number of women testing positive in Test A. Thus, we simply calculate 63 x (20/45) = 28. Thus, we expect that 28 women actually have Kryptos Virus.

Question 21: B
In total 108 people tested positive under test A, and 49 of these tested positive under test B (using the data given in the last question). Therefore the percentage of people positive in Test A also testing positive in Test B is 49 out of 108, which is 45.4%.

SET 6
Question 22: B
The cost of the plan is 190 + 600 + 140 = 930 R per day

Question 23: C

Firstly we need to find the two options that save the most money, aside from the one already stated. The two best options are to send material from Warehouse A to Store 1, and material from Warehouse B to store 2. We can see from the table that these 2 options will be 30 R per day cheaper than sending from Warehouse A to store 2, and Warehouse B to store 1 (as with the current business plan).

The new total cost is 100 + 180 + 450 = 730 R. Thus the saving is (930 – 730) = 200 R. 200 R is 22% of 930 R, so the percentage saving is 22% (to the nearest whole number).

SET 7

Question 24: B

The shop sold 512 books outside of the visit event (sum of sales in the table), and 106 at the event.

Thus the percentage at the event was 106/(512+106) = 17%.

Question 25: B

Firstly calculate the different revenues:

Non-fiction revenue = (12+30) x£10 = £420

Fiction revenue = (50+45+23+90+103+159) x£6 = £2,820

Then calculate the non-fiction percentage: 420/(2,820+420) = 13%.

Question 26: B

The weekly revenue is seven times the daily revenue.

Daily revenue from Fiction: (50+45+23+90+103+159) x£6 = £2,820.

Daily revenue from Non-fiction 2x(12+30) x£10 = £840.

Therefore weekly revenue is 7x(£28.20+£840) = £25,620.

Question 27: D

The shop's revenue is now £6 x (100+90+23+90+103+159) + £10 x (12+30) per day. This income equates to £3,810 per day and £26,670 per week.

Therefore the percentage difference is 26,670/25,620 = 1.04, giving a 4% increase on the previous week.

SET 8
Question 28: B
2 nights in Venice in a 3 star hotel, I room (the children are exempt) = 2x1x3 = 6 euros
2 nights in Rome in a 3 star hotel, 3 people paying (the child aged 9 is exempt) = 2x3x5 = 30 Euros
2 nights in Padua in a 3 star hotel, 2 people paying (both children exempt) = 2x2x2 = 8 euros
2 nights in Siena in the high season, 3 paying (child aged 9 exempt) = 2x3x2 = 12 euros
So the entire cost is the sum of these costs = 6+30+8+12 = 56 euros.

Question 29: B
In Rome he pays 6 euros x 7 nights = 42 Euros. In Padua he pays 3 euros x 8 nights = 24 Euros. 42:24 = 7:4.

Question 30: B
A 3 star hotel in Venice for 2 days costs Alice 6 Euros. 3 days in a 4 star hotel in Padua costs 9 Euros. This is 50% more in Padua than in Venice.

Question 31: C
The maximum cost of tax in a 4 star hotel in Rome is 6 euros x 10 nights = 60 EUR. Up until this point it will always be cheaper in Padua. In Padua the cost for a 4 star hotel is 3 euros a night, therefore after 20 days the cost of the Padua hotel is equal to the cost of a stay of equivalent duration in Rome.

SET 9
Question 32: C
Emissions increased by 1,000 tonnes from 1,000 to 2,000 tonnes over 5 years, therefore the rate of increase was 200 tonnes per year

Question 33: A
If there had been no crash, 2,010 emissions would have been 3,000 Tonnes, as calculated by applying an increase in emissions of 200 Tonnes/year from 2005 to 2010.
With the economic crash, 2010 emissions were 2500 Tonnes:
3,000 – 2,500 = 500 Tonnes less in 2010 due to the economic crash.

Question 34: C

Percentage increase = (new amount – old amount)/old amount x 100
= (3,000–2,000)/2,000 x 100 = 50%.

Note that you are asked for the percentage INCREASE. (New amount/old amount) x100 = percentage CHANGE.

Question 35: B

2015 – 2020 the amount would increase from 3,000 tonnes to 3,500 tonnes without any action. This equates to a rate of increase of 100 tonnes per year. With the new act, this is reduced by 50% to 50 tonnes per year, thus over 5 years: Overall saving = 50 x 5 = 250 Tonnes

SET 10

Question 36: D

We can calculate the number of people who reacted positively in each group and then add up the total:
75% of 300 is 225
65% of 300 is 195
70% of 300 is 210
55% of 300 is 165
225 + 195 + 210 + 165 = 795

Question 37: C

In group 2, 30% reacted negatively: 30% of 300 is 90.
In group 3, 15% reacted negatively: 15% of 300 is 45.
Therefore the difference is 45; 45 more people in group 2 reacted negatively than people in group 3.

Question 38: B

We can calculate the number of people who reacted negatively in each group and then add up the total:
20% of 300 is 60
30% of 300 is 90
15% of 300 is 45
25% of 300 is 75
60 + 90 + 45 + 75 = 270
270 as a percentage of the total, 1200, is 22.5%, which rounds to 23%.

Question 39: D
The overall success rate of the first four groups was = (75 + 65 + 70 + 55)/4
= 66.25%
Therefore increase in success rate = 82/66.25 = 23.77% increase.

Question 40: B
In the answer to question 143 we calculated that in the first 4 groups, 270 people reacted negatively. In group 5, 15% of 300 people, which is 45 people, reacted negatively. Hence the negative reactions total 315 people.

SET 11
Question 41: C
4 tablespoons is 4 x 15 ml = 60 ml. 250 ml is 1 cup, so 4 tablespoons is 60 ml/250 ml = 0.24 cups. 2 cups + 1 cup + ½ cup + 0.24 cups = 3.74 cups.

Question 42: A
First calculate the weight of butter called for by the recipe:
4 tablespoons = 60 ml = 0.06 litres = 0.06 dm^3 (the question states that 1dm^3
= 1 litre).
Weight of butter: 950 grams/dm^3 x 0.06 dm^3 = 57 grams.

Next, calculate the weight of milk called for by the recipe:
½ cup = 1.25 dl = 0.125 litres = 0.125 dm^3.
Weight of milk: 1050 grams/dm^3 x 0.125 dm^3 = 131.25 grams.

Question 43: E
Any whole number multiple of flour, sugar or milk can be measured with a ½ cup.

4 tablespoons is 60 ml, ½ cup is 125 ml. The least common multiple of 60 and 125 is 1500, representing the smallest possible amount of butter that can be measured with half-cup measures.

1500 grams of butter makes 25 batches of muffins, which would require 25 x 2 cups = 50 cups of flour.
Thus, the weight ratio of Milk:Butter is 131.25/57:1 = 2.3:1.

Question 44: A

The recipe will have:

2 cups of milk = 500 ml = 0.5 dm³

1 cup of sugar = 250 ml = 0.25 dm³

½ cup of flour = 125 ml = 0.125 dm³

4 tablespoons of butter = 60 ml = 0.06 dm³.

Therefore the volume of the batter is 0.5 dm³ + 0.25 dm³ + 0.125 dm³ + 0.06 dm³ = 0.935 dm³.

Now, to calculate the density of the batter, multiply the density of each ingredient by the proportion of the batter it makes up, and then add up these figures, as follows:

(1050 grams/dm³ milk x 0.5/0.935) + (850 grams/dm³ sugar x 0.25/0.935) + (600 grams/dm³ flour x 0.125/0.935) + (950 grams/dm³ butter x 0.06/0.935) = 561.5 grams/dm³ + 227.3 grams/dm³ + 80.2 grams/dm³ + 61.0 grams/dm³ = 930 grams/dm³

Question 45: E

10 muffins x 100 grams = 1,000 grams batter required.

The recipe calls for:

2 cups flour = 5 dl = 0.5 dm³ flour. Weight of the flour is 0.5 dm³ x 600 grams/dm³ = 300 grams.

1 cup sugar = 2.5 dl = 0.25 dm³ sugar. Weight of the sugar is 0.25 dm³ x 850 grams/dm³ = 212.5 grams.

From question 42 we remember that the weight of the milk as called for by the recipe is 131.25 grams and weight of the butter is 57 grams.

Thus the overall weight of the batter is 300 + 212.5 + 131.25 + 57 = 700.75 grams.

700.75/1,000 grams batter = 57/B grams butter, where B is the amount of butter required in 1,000g batter. B = 81.3 grams butter.

Question 46: C

700.75/1,000 grams batter = 300/F grams flour, where F is the amount of flour required to make 1,000 grams of muffin. F = 428.11 grams. 428.11 grams/1000 grams = 0.428 = 43 % to the nearest whole number.

SET 12

Question 47: A

The trend shows a 10 km^2 decrease in thickness for every 100 °C decrease in temperature. 10 km^2 thickness is 1,300 °C, so extrapolating the trend gives 0 km^2 thickness at 1,200 °C.

Question 48: D

Spreading rate is not affected by temperature, it is an independent variable. This question is designed to test your attention to detail and reinforce the importance of reading questions properly. Ensure you constantly pay attention to what the question is asking.

Question 49: D

Crustal volume per year = 20 km^2 crustal thickness x 20 mm/year spreading rate x 1 year = 20,000,000,000,000 mm^2 x 20 mm = 400,000,000,000,000 mm^3 = 400,000 m^3

Question 50: C

In answering this question, it is not necessary to use the same units for crustal thickness and spreading rate, as long as we use the same units for the crustal thickness *from both locations*, and likewise for the spreading rate.

Location A = 10 x 100 = 1,000. Location C = 30 x 150 = 4,500. A:C = 1:4,500/1,000 = 1:4.5

Question 51: A

Crustal volume per time = crustal thickness x spreading rate.
Crustal thickness at E is 10 km^2 and at F is 25 km^2.
Crustal volume per time is equal, so 10 km^2 x spreading rate E = 25 km^2 x spreading rate F. Therefore the spreading rate at E = 2.5 the spreading rate at F. Thus, it is 250 % faster.

Question 52: E

Temperature at D is 1,600 °C, decreased by 10 % it would be 1440 °C.
From the trend in temperature and crustal thickness this corresponds to a crustal thickness of 24 km^2.
Crustal volume per 3 years = 24 km^2 crustal thickness x 50 mm/year x 3 years = 24,000,000,000,000 mm^2 x 150 mm = 3,600,000,000,000,000 mm^3

SET 13

Question 53: C

A: 9/25, B: 6/23, C: 7/22, D: 8/24. (9+6+7+8)/(25+23+22+24) = 30/94 = 32 %
to the nearest whole number.

Question 54: E

In Group A, drug-takers visual accuracy is 36%/27% = 33.33% improved.
In Group C, drug-takers visual accuracy is 31%/29% = 6.90% improved.
A:C = 33.33%/6.90%:1 = 4.83:1.

Question 55: C

10 women and 15 men have 45 % and unknown (P %) accuracy, respectively.
All 25 have an average of 36 % accuracy.
(10/25 x 45) + (15/25 x P) = 36.
P=30.

Question 56: A

Diabetics with vision problems correspond to Group A. In Group A, 15 of 25
volunteers reported better vision after taking the drug, but 9 of 25 volunteers
taking a placebo also reported vision improvement. This suggests only 6 of 25
had reported improvements in their vision thanks to the effects of the drug.

6/25 x 100,000 people = 24,000 people.

Question 57: D

The placebo group showed no change, so only the volunteers being affected
by the drug compound will see greater improvements to their vision.
15 – 9 = 6 volunteers affected by drug originally.
200% of the dose gave (18-9)/6 = 1.5 = 150 % the number of people with drug-
related improvements.
300% of the dose will thus give 300 % / 200 % x 150 % = 225 % the number of
people.
6 volunteers x 225% = 13.5 volunteers. (9+13.5)/25 volunteers = 22.5/25
volunteers = 90.0 % of volunteers.

Question 58: D

D is supported, because in all groups taking the placebo, there was an increase in accuracy with reading letters, suggesting better vision, and in many cases this was equivalent to the increase in those taking the drug.

The data suggest that A) and B) are incorrect. Only one group showed a higher increase in accuracy amongst the placebo group, in all other groups the people taking the drug had a larger % increase in accuracy. In healthy volunteers, there was as much of an increase in accuracy amongst those taking a placebo, suggesting the drug does not have as much of an effect in healthy volunteers. Options C) and E) are relatively meaningless statements which are not supported by the data.

SET 14

Question 59: C

5 calories x 200 pounds x 1 hour = 1000 calories running.
Cycling burns 50 calories + (5 calories x -5) for each mile = 25 calories per mile. Cycling 5 miles gives a total burn 125 calories, which is less than the amount burned running.

Thus, the maximum calorie burn comes from running, which will burn 1000 calories.

Question 60: D

Losing 10 pounds requires a 35 000 calorie deficit.
30 min run: 200 pounds x 0.5 hours x 5 calories = 500 calories.
20 mile cycle at 20 mph: 50 calories + (5 calories/mph x 10 mph) = 100 calories/mile for 20 miles = 2,000 calories. Daily burn is 2500 calories. 35,000/2,000 calories per day = 14 days taken to lose 10 pounds.

Question 61: C

Both their weight loss goal and calories burned running are linearly proportional to weight. Thus, they need to run for the same amount of time in order to achieve their goals.

Question 62: A
10% of 140 pounds is 14 pounds of weight, thus this is how much weight she wishes to lose.
At 3,500 calories/pound she needs a 14 pounds x 3500 calories/pound = 49,000 calorie deficit.

Her BMR is 1500 calories and she eats 400+500+250+200=1,350 calories per day, so her daily calorie deficit is 1,500 calories-1,350 calories = 150 calories.

It will take her 49 000 calories/150 calories per day = 326.67 days to reach her goal (327 to the nearest day).

Question 63: E
10 miles at 10 mph: 50 calories + (5 calories x 0 mph) = 50 calories/mile for 10 miles = 500 calories.

She requires a 49,000 calorie deficit, as worked out in the previous question. Previously she had a daily deficit of 150 calories, now she has a daily deficit of 650 calories. Thus, she now has a calorie deficit which is 4.33 times the previous deficit, so she will reach her goal 4.33 times faster.

Question 64: E
1 chocolate is the least she can eat, which means she eats 3 pieces of chicken and 6 bowls of cereal.
1x350 calories + 3x250 calories + 6x400 calories = 3,500 calories.

The lowest calorie arrangement of the 3 other foods is 1 lasagna, 3 vegetables and 6 apples.
1x700 calories + 3x200 calories + 6x100 calories = 1,900 calories.

She has a 3,500 calories per day – 1500 calorie BMR = 2,000 calorie surplus before and 400 calorie surplus after. 2,000 calories:400 calories = 5:1.

SET 15
Question 65: C
In 2011-2012, food grain production was 100, and this was a 25% increase on 2010-2011.
If 100 is 125%, then 100% = 80. Hence food production in tonnes in 2010-2011 was 80 tonnes.

Question 66: B
Target production (2011-12) = 60 tonnes
Actual production (2010-11) = 50/125% = 40 tonnes
Difference = 60 - 40 = 20 tonnes

Question 67: B
Difference = Target - Actual = 50 - 40 = 10 tonnes

Question 68: D
Cotton production (2010-11) = 30/120% = 25 tonnes
Jute production (2010-11) = 20/125% = 16 tonnes
Combined = 25 + 16 = 41 tonnes

Question 69: D
Food grain production (2010-11) = 100/125% = 80 tonnes
Oil seeds production (2010-11) = 50/125% = 40 tonnes
Difference = 80 - 40 = 40 tonnes

SET 16
Question 70: D
Sales of product B in Feb = 7,000
Total sales of all products in Feb = 10,250 + 7,000 + 3,750 + 3100 = 24,100
Percentage of product B's sales = 7,000/24,100 = 29%

Question 71: D
Percentage increase:
Product A = (11,000-10,500)/10,500 = 4.76%
Product B = (7,500-7,250)/7,250 = 3.45%
Product C = (4,250-4,000)/4,000 = 6.25%
Product D = (4,000-3,500)/3,500 = 14.29%

Hence product D witnessed highest percentage growth. However to answer this question more quickly, look at the numbers – the numbers are giving you a clue. You can visually see that product D's sales' values have gone up the equal maximum amount of £500. But it is also apparent that the absolute value of sales is the lowest, therefore you can deduce that D is the largest percentage increase without actually doing any sums!

Question 72: C

Sales of product C in May = 4,250 × 1.2 = 5,100
Therefore sales of product D in May = 5,100
Percentage increase in sales of D from April to May = (5,100 − 4,000)/4,000 = 27.5%

Question 73: D

Sale of products (A+C) in January = 13,000
Sale of products (A+C) in April = 15,250
Percentage increase in combined sale from January to April = (15,250 − 13,000)/13,000 = 17.31%

Question 74: A

Sale of product (A+B) in May = 1.2 × (11,000+75,00) = 22,200
Sale of product (C+D) in May = 1.3 × (4,250+4,000) = 10,725
Total sales in May = 32925

SET 17

Question 75: A

This is a difficult question that would be worth "flagging for review". Set the percentage of lead in alloy A to a, and the percentage of tin in alloy C to b. We can then find the percentage of copper in each as a function of a and b.

Alloy	Zinc	Tin	Lead	Copper	Nickel
A	10%	40%	a%	(40-a)%	10%
B	25%	15%	50%	5%	5%
C	15%	b%	20%	(30-b)%	35%

The key thing here is to use the composition of Alloy G. We can find the composition of Alloy G in terms of a and b and then set the amounts of tin, lead and copper equal to each other to find a and b:

For Alloy G, the percentages will be weighted according to the proportion A:B:C = 2:1:3:

2/6 (40) + 1/6 (15) + 3/6 (b) = 2/6 (a) + 1/6 (50) + 3/6 (20) = 2/6 (40-a) + 1/6 (5) + 3/6 (30-b)
80 + 15 + 3b = 2a + 50 + 60 = 80 -2a + 5 + 90 -3b

Solving above equation, we will get values:

$95 + 3b = 2a + 110$

$2a + 110 = 175 - 2a - 3b$

$3b = 65 - 4a$

$2a = 95 - 110 + 65 - 4a$

$6a = 50$

$a = 50/6$

$b = 95/9$

Percentage of Lead in alloy A = a = 50/6% = 25/3% = 8.33%

Question 76: C

Using our solution from the previous question, we found that the percentage of Tin in alloy C, b, was:

$b = 95/9$

Percentage of Tin in alloy C = 95/9 = 10.6%

Question 77: B

Zinc percentage in alloy X is equal to the average of the percentages of the composite alloys, as they are present in equal proportions. This can be found by adding together and dividing by 3.

X = (10+25+15)/3 = 50/3 = 16.67%

Question 78: D

To solve, subtract the amounts of the known metals to find the remaining metal, which is equal to the percentage of Tin and Copper combined in alloy C. We know there are no other components as this is stated in the question.

(100% - 15% - 20% - 35%) = 30%

Question 79: B

We know the percentages of tin in each of the alloys which make up Alloy G, and the composition of Alloy G. Alloy G is made up of alloys A:B:C in the ratio 2:1:3. Alloy A has 40% tin, alloy B has 15% and alloy C has 95/9% tin. Hence the percentage in Alloy G is (2/6 x 40)+(1/6 x 15)+(3/6 x 95/9) = 21.11%.

Question 80: C

Percentage of elements in alloy G:

We know that Alloy G has 21.11% Tin from the last question. We also know from the initial explanation that it has the same concentration of tin, lead and copper. This is 3 elements with the same concentration. We then need to work out how much nickel and zinc there is to check whether there is a 4th.

Alloy G is made up of alloys A:B:C in the ratio 2:1:3. Alloy A has 10% nickel, alloy B has 5% and alloy C has 35% nickel. Hence the percentage in Alloy G is ((2x10)+(1x5)+(3x35))/6, = 21.6666.

We can also work out from the fact that these 4 elements plus Zinc are 100% of the total that Zinc is 15%.

Zinc = 15%
Tin = 21.11%
Lead = 21.11%
Copper = 21.11%
Nickel = 21.67%

SET 18
Question 81: B
The easiest way to solve this problem is using a Venn diagram. The Venn diagram below shows all possible combinations of the three devices each student can have as well as the number of students with a combination of devices. The sum of the numbers in the Venn diagram must be equal to the total number of students.

Using the information given in the graphs, we know there are:

- 30 students with all three devices
- 50 students with smartphone only
- 40 students with tablet only
- 50 students with laptop only
- 180 students with smartphone
- 190 students with tablet
- 200 students with laptop

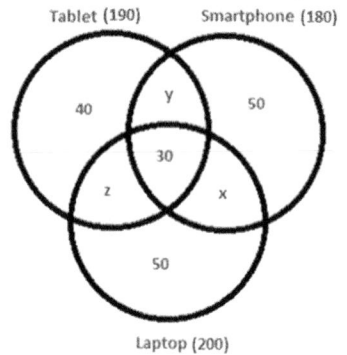

Therefore we can construct the following Venn diagram:

Laptop: $200=50+30+z+x \rightarrow z=120-x$
Smartphone: $180 =50+30+x+y \rightarrow y=100-x$
Tablet: $190=40+30+y+z \rightarrow y=120-z$

So, we see that $y=100-x$ and $y=120-z$ and thus $z=20+x$
Then, we see that $z=20+x$ and $z=120-x$ and thus $x=50$
Plug it in to see, $z=20+x=70$ and $y=100-x=50$

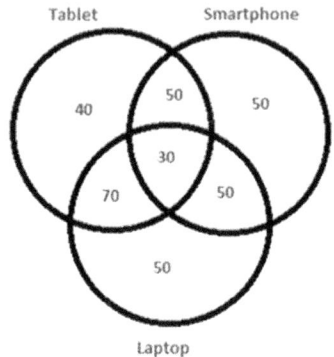

Now, the total number of students is the sum of the numbers in the Venn diagram.

Question 82: C
Using the previously constructed Venn diagram, we can see the total number of students with a smartphone and a laptop is 50.

Question 83: A
180 students have smartphone
100 students have both tablet and laptop
So, 180-100=80, 80 students.

Question 84: C
Total number of students: 340
80 students have both smartphone and laptop.
80/340=0.25 → 23.5%

Question 85: C
185/345=0.536 → 54%
185 – no of students with smartphone (AFTER)
345 – total no of students (AFTER)

BEFORE

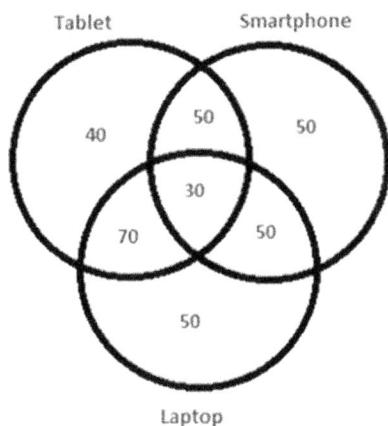

AFTER

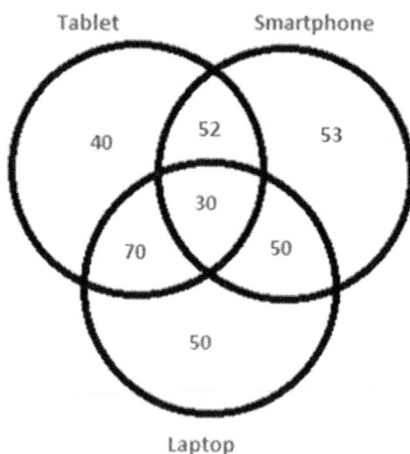

SET 19

Question 86: B

Davos: 15cm, 15cm, 15cm and 10cm in November, December, January, February respectively

Chamonix Mont-Blanc: 5cm, 40cm, 15cm, 20cm in November, December, January, February respectively

We can use these figures to create the equation:

$(15+15+15+10)+(5+40+15+20)/8=16.875$ cm

Question 87: C

Davos: 15cm, 15cm, 15cm and 10cm in November, December, January, February respectively

Average snowfall in Davos: $(15+15+15+10)/4 = 13.75$

Chamonix Mont-Blanc: 5cm, 40cm, 15cm, 20cm in November, December, January, February respectively

Average snowfall in Chamonix Mont-Blanc: $(5+40+15+20)/4 =20$

Cortina d' Ampezzo: 50cm, 50cm, 40cm and 5cm in November, December, January, February respectively

Average snowfall in Cortina d' Ampezzo: (50+50+40+5)/4=36.25
Garmisch Partenkirchen: 10cm, 15cm, 35cm, 20cm in November, December, January, February respectively
Average snowfall in Garmisch Partenkirchen: (10+15+35+20)/4=20
So the highest average snowfall was in Cotine d'Ampezzo.

Question 88: C
Inserting figures from all of the places into an equation:
December/February = (15+15+50+40)/(35+10+40+20)=120/105=1.14

Question 89: B
We are told that in November 2014 there is 30cm of snowfall (in all four areas)
To work out November 2015, we need to add all the areas: - Garmisch-Partenkirchen: 10cm, Davos: 15cm, Cortina d'Ampezzo: 5cm, Chamonix Mont-Blanc: 5cm
This gives us 35cm for November 2015
This gives us the equation: 35/30=1.1667

Question 90: D
We need to add the values for November and February for both of these places.
Cortina d' Ampezzo 5 + 40 = 45
Garmisch Partenkirchen 35 + 10 = 45
Sum: 45 + 45 = 90

SET 20
Question 91: C
Total number of people aged under 22 = sum of first two columns = 62
Number aged <22 who spotted >10 differences = 11 + 8 + 3 + 2 = 24
Percentage = 24/62 = 38.7

Question 92: D
Valid results for 5-10 spots for ages 16-22 = 0.25 x 12 = 3
Total number of valid results for 16-22 = 10 + 3 + 8 + 2 = 23
Percentage of over 15 spots for 16-22 = 2 ÷ 23 = 8.7%

Question 93: C
Total who spotted over 10 = sum of bottom two rows = 52
25% of 52 = 13

Question 94: E
Total 48+ who spotted <5 = 15 + 19 = 34
Total aged 48+ = sum of final two columns = 66
Percentage of 48+ who spotted <5 = 34 ÷ 66 = 52% (2 s.f.)
52% of 10,000 = 0.52 x 10,000 = 5,200

Question 95: E
50% increase in 16-34s who spot 11-15 = 1.5 x (8 + 6) = 21
New total who spot 11-15 = 11 + 21 + 2 + 8 + 9 = 51
Ratio = 21:51

SET 21
Question 96: B
Number that play Football = 22% of 1300 = 286
Number that play Hockey = 8 % of 1300 = 104
Thus, the difference = 286-104 = 182 Boys + Girls; Therefore, 182/2 = 91 Boys

Question 97: D
22% of 350 = 77 students
77 ÷ 11 people per team = 7 teams

Question 98: C
Number of basketball boys = 0.05 x 1,300 = 65
80% of 65 = 52
Number of netball girls = 0.08 x1, 300 = 104
Total number of netball-players = 104 + 52 = 156
Male proportion = 52 ÷ 156 = 33% (2 s.f.)

Question 99: D
Number of *Other* students = 0.12 x 1,300 = 156
Other ball sports = 0.25 x 156 = 39
Total non-ball sports (swimming & athletics) = (0.06 + 0.03) x 1300 = 117
Total "other" non ball sports = 156 – 39 = 117
Total ball sports = 1,300 – 117 – 117 = 1,066

Question 100: A

Girls who play hockey = 0.07 x 1,300 = 91

Boys who play cricket = 0.1 x 1,300 = 130

Difference = 39. *Note the tennis info makes no difference (50:50 split)*

SET 22
Question 101: A

Total apples processed in 1998 = 1,100,547 + 2,983,411 = 4,083,958

Total apples processed in 2003 = 1,931,784 + 2,439,012 = 4,370,796

Ratio = 4,370,796 ÷ 4,083,958 = 1.07 (i.e. 7% increase)

Question 102: E

Number of No Goods in worst year = 571,221

Total number of No Goods = sum of bottom row = 2,823,732

Percentage = 571,221 ÷ 2,823,732 = 20.2% (3 s.f.)

Question 103: A

2004 total No Goods = 3 x 571,221 = 1,713,663

70% of edible apples are processed, as are all passable apples.

Difference = (0.7 x 1,931,784 + 2,439,012) − 1,713,663 = 2,077,598

Question 104: C

Total number of edibles 1998-2003 = sum of top row = 9,201,790

20% increase = 1.2 x 9,201,790 = 11,042,148

30% of these are sold as they come = 0.3 x 11,042,148 = 3,312,644

Question 105: B

Apples processed for cider = (1,931,784 x 0.7) + 2,439,012 = 3,791,260.8

Litres of cider = 3,791,260.80 ÷ 20 = 189,600 litres (4 s.f.)

SET 23
Question 106: C

Decreased average speed = 0.92 x 5 mph = 4.6 mph

Miles covered = 4.6 x (40 ÷ 60) = 3.07 miles

Km covered = 1.6 x 3.07 miles = 4.9 km

Question 107: C
Distance per session = 26 miles ÷ 4 = 6.5 miles
Time per session = 6.5 miles ÷ 5 mph = 1.3 hrs = 1hr 18mins

Question 108: B
New wet average speed = 0.92 x 4.6 mph = 4.232 mph
12 km in miles = 12 km ÷ 1.6 = 7.5 miles
Time taken = 7.5 miles ÷ 4.232 mph = 1.77 hrs = 1hr 46mins

Question 109: B
Distance of second jog = 4 km x 1.5 = 6 km
Distance of third jog = 6 km x 1.5 = 9 km
Distance of last jog = 9 km x 1.5 = 13.5 km
13.5 km in miles = 13.5 km ÷ 1.6 = 8.4375 miles
Time = 8.4375 miles ÷ 5 mph = 1.69 hrs = 1hr 41mins

Question 110: C
3hrs 42mins = 3.7 hrs
Average speed = 26 miles ÷ 3.7 hrs = 7.027 mph
7.027 mph ÷ 5 mph = 1.405 (i.e. 41% increase)

SET 24
Question 111: D
Psychology: 10/6 = 1.66
To determine the course with a similar ratio of men to women as psychology, we need to calculate the ratios for all of the other courses
Mathematics: 8/7 =1.14
Physics: 10/15 = 0.66
Programming: 4/5 = 0.8
Literature: 12/8 = 1.5
History: 7/7 =1
From these figures, we can see that Literature has the most similar ratio.

Question 112: C

Physics: $10/15 = 0.66$

Similarly to the previous question, we need to calculate the ratios for all other courses

Psychology: $10/6 = 1.66$

Mathematics: $8/7 = 1.14$

Programming: $4/5 = 0.8$

Literature: $12/8 = 1.5$

History: $7/7 = 1$

Question 113: E

Can't tell because students can take more than one course.

Question 114: E

As one student can take more than one course and we do not have any information about the total number of students we cannot say.

Question 115: C

Before ratio: $10{:}6 = (10/6){:}1 = 1.66{:}1$

After ratio: $13{:}6 = (13/6){:}1 = 2.16{:}1$

Difference: $2.16{-}1.66 = 0.5$

MATHEMATICS: ANSWER KEY

Question	Answer	Question	Answer	Question	Answer
1	B	26	B	51	D
2	C	27	A	52	D
3	C	28	F	53	B
4	C	29	D	54	E
5	E	30	A	55	E
6	A	31	D	56	B
7	C	32	D	57	C
8	E	33	F	58	A
9	E	34	B	59	C
10	C	35	C	60	B
11	E	36	B	61	B
12	E	37	C	62	B
13	E	38	A	63	C
14	B	39	A	64	C
15	C	40	C	65	A
16	B	41	B	66	C
17	B	42	D	67	D
18	C	43	C	68	C
19	D	44	A	69	D
20	C	45	C	70	A
21	B	46	C	71	C
22	A	47	C	72	B
23	F	48	B	73	B
24	D	49	D	74	A
25	A	50	E	75	C

MATHEMATICS: WORKED ANSWERS

Question 1: B

Each three-block combination is mutually exclusive to any other combination, so the probabilities are added. Each block pick is independent of all other picks, so the probabilities can be multiplied. For this scenario there are three possible combinations:

P(2 red blocks and 1 yellow block) = P(red then red then yellow) + P(red then yellow then red) + P(yellow then red then red) =

$$(\frac{12}{20} \times \frac{11}{19} \times \frac{8}{18}) + (\frac{12}{20} \times \frac{8}{19} \times \frac{11}{18}) + (\frac{8}{20} \times \frac{12}{19} \times \frac{11}{18}) =$$

$$\frac{3 \times 12 \times 11 \times 8}{20 \times 19 \times 18} = \frac{44}{95}$$

Question 2: C

Multiply through by 15: $3(3x + 5) + 5(2x - 2) = 18 \times 15$

Thus: $9x + 15 + 10x - 10 = 270$

$9x + 10x = 270 - 15 + 10$

$19x = 265$

$x = 13.95$

Question 3: C

This is a rare case where you need to factorise a complex polynomial:

(3x)(x) = 0, possible pairs: 2 x 10, 10 x 2, 4 x 5, 5 x 4

(3x - 4)(x + 5) = 0

3x - 4 = 0, so x = $\frac{4}{3}$

x + 5 = 0, so x = -5

Question 4: C

$$\frac{5(x-4)}{(x+2)(x-4)} + \frac{3(x+2)}{(x+2)(x-4)}$$

$$= \frac{5x-20+3x+6}{(x+2)(x-4)}$$

$$= \frac{8x-14}{(x+2)(x-4)}$$

Question 5: E

$p \alpha \sqrt[3]{q}$, so $p = k \sqrt[3]{q}$

$p = 12$ when $q = 27$ gives $12 = k \sqrt[3]{27}$, so $12 = 3k$ and $k = 4$

so $p = 4 \sqrt[3]{q}$

Now $p = 24$:

$24 = 4\sqrt[3]{q}$, so $6 = \sqrt[3]{q}$ and $q = 6^3 = 216$

Question 6: A

$8 \times 9 = 72$

$8 = (4 \times 2) = 2 \times 2 \times 2$

$9 = 3 \times 3$

$(2 \times 2 \times 2 \times 3 \times 3)^2 = 2 \times 2 \times 2 \times 2 \times 2 \times 2 \times 3 \times 3 \times 3 \times 3 = 2^6 \times 3^4$

Question 7: C

Note that $1.151 \times 2 = 2.302$.

Thus: $\frac{2 \times 10^5 + 2 \times 10^2}{10^{10}} = 2 \times 10^{-5} + 2 \times 10^{-8}$

$= 0.00002 + 0.00000002 = 0.00002002$

Question 8: E

$y^2 + ay + b$

$= (y + 2)^2 - 5 = y^2 + 4y + 4 - 5$

$= y^2 + 4y + 4 - 5 = y^2 + 4y - 1$

So $a = 4$ and $y = -1$

Question 9: E

Take $5(m + 4n)$ as a common factor to give: $\frac{4(m+4n)}{5(m+4n)} + \frac{5(m-2n)}{5(m+4n)}$

Simplify to give: $\frac{4m+16n+5m-10n}{5(m+4n)} = \frac{9m+6n}{5(m+4n)} = \frac{3(3m+2n)}{5(m+4n)}$

Question 10: C

$A \alpha \frac{1}{\sqrt{B}}$. Thus, $= \frac{k}{\sqrt{B}}$.

Substitute the values in to give: $4 = \frac{k}{\sqrt{25}}$.

Thus, $k = 20$.

Therefore, $A = \frac{20}{\sqrt{B}}$.

When B = 16, $A = \frac{20}{\sqrt{16}} = \frac{20}{4} = 5$

Question 11: E
Angles SVU and STU are opposites and add up to 180°, so STU = 91°
The angle of the centre of a circle is twice the angle at the circumference so SOU = 2 x 91° = 182°

Question 12: E
The surface area of an open cylinder A = 2πrh. Cylinder B is an enlargement of A, so the increases in radius (r) and height (h) will be proportional: $\frac{r_A}{r_B} = \frac{h_A}{h_B}$.

Let us call the proportion coefficient n, where n = $\frac{r_A}{r_B} = \frac{h_A}{h_B}$.

So $\frac{Area\ A}{Area\ B} = \frac{2\pi r_A h_A}{2\pi r_B h_B} = n\ x\ n = n^2$. $\frac{Area\ A}{Area\ B} = \frac{32\pi}{8\pi} = 4$, so n = 2.

The proportion coefficient n = 2 also applies to their volumes, where the third dimension (also radius, i.e. the r^2 in V = $\pi r^2 h$) is equally subject to this constant of proportionality. The cylinder's volumes are related by $n^3 = 8$.

If the smaller cylinder has volume 2π cm³, then the larger will have volume 2π x n^3 = 2π x 8 = 16π cm³.

Question 13: E
$$= \frac{8}{x(3-x)} - \frac{6(3-x)}{x(3-x)}$$

$$= \frac{8-18+6x}{x(3-x)}$$

$$= \frac{6x-10}{x(3-x)}$$

Question 14: B
For the black ball to be drawn in the last round, white balls must be drawn every round. Thus the probability is given by

$$P = \frac{9}{10}\ x\ \frac{8}{9}\ x\ \frac{7}{8}\ x\ \frac{6}{7}\ x\ \frac{5}{6}\ x\ \frac{4}{5}\ x\ \frac{3}{4}\ x\ \frac{2}{3}\ x\ \frac{1}{2}$$

$$= \frac{9\ x\ 8\ x\ 7\ x\ 6\ x\ 5\ x\ 4\ x\ 3\ x\ 2\ x\ 1}{10\ x\ 9\ x\ 8\ x\ 7\ x\ 6\ x\ 5\ x\ 4\ x\ 3\ x\ 2\ x\ 1} = \frac{1}{10}$$

155

Question 15: C

The probability of getting a king the first time is $\frac{4}{52} = \frac{1}{13}$, and the probability of getting a king the second time is $\frac{3}{51}$. These are independent events, thus, the probability of drawing two kings is $\frac{1}{13} x \frac{3}{51} = \frac{3}{663} = \frac{1}{221}$

Question 16: B

The probabilities of all outcomes must sum to one, so if the probability of rolling a 1 is x, then: $x + x + x + x + 2x = 1$. Therefore, $x = \frac{1}{7}$.

The probability of obtaining two sixes $P_{12} = \frac{2}{7} x \frac{2}{7} = \frac{4}{49}$

Question 17: B

There are plenty of ways of counting, however the easiest is as follows: 0 is divisible by both 2 and 3. Half of the numbers from 1 to 36 are even (i.e. 18 of them). 3, 9, 15, 21, 27, 33 are the only numbers divisible by 3 that we've missed. There are 25 outcomes divisible by 2 or 3, out of 37.

Question 18: C

List the six ways of achieving this outcome: HHTT, HTHT, HTTH, TTHH, THTH, and THHT. There are 2^4 possible outcomes for 4 consecutive coin flips, so the probability of two heads and two tails is: $6 x \frac{1}{2^4} = \frac{6}{16} = \frac{3}{8}$

Question 19: D

Count the number of ways to get a 5, 6 or 7 (draw the square if helpful). The ways to get a 5 are: 1, 4; 2, 3; 3, 2; 4, 1. The ways to get a 6 are: 1, 5; 2, 4; 3, 3; 4, 2; 5, 1. The ways to get a 7 are: 1, 6; 2, 5; 3, 4; 4, 3; 5, 2; 6, 1. That is 15 out of 36 possible outcomes.

	1	2	3	4	5	6
1	2	3	4	5	6	7
2	3	4	5	6	7	8
3	4	5	6	7	8	9
4	5	6	7	8	9	10
5	6	7	8	9	10	11
6	7	8	9	10	11	12

Question 20: C

There are x+y+z balls in the bag, and the probability of picking a red ball is $\frac{x}{(x+y+z)}$ and the probability of picking a green ball is $\frac{z}{(x+y+z)}$. These are independent events, so the probability of picking red then green is $\frac{xz}{(x+y+z)^2}$ and the probability of picking green then red is the same. These outcomes are mutually exclusive, so are added.

Question 21: B

There are two ways of doing it, pulling out a red ball then a blue ball, or pulling out a blue ball and then a red ball. Let us work out the probability of the first: $\frac{x}{(x+y+z)} \times \frac{y}{x+y+z-1}$, and the probability of the second option will be the same. These are mutually exclusive options, so the probabilities may be summed.

Question 22: A

[x: Player 1 wins point, y: Player 2 wins point]
Player 1 wins in five rounds if we get: yxxxx, xyxxx, xxyxx, xxxyx.
(Note the case of xxxxy would lead to player 1 winning in 4 rounds, which the question forbids.)
Each of these have a probability of $p^4(1-p)$. Thus, the solution is $4p^4(1-p)$.

Question 23: F

$4x + 7 + 18x + 20 = 14$
$22x + 27 = 14$
Thus, $22x = -13$
Giving $x = -\frac{13}{22}$

Question 24: D

$$r^3 = \frac{3V}{4\pi}$$

Thus, $r = \left(\frac{3V}{4\pi}\right)^{1/3}$

Therefore, $S = 4\pi\left[\left(\frac{3V}{4\pi}\right)^{\frac{1}{3}}\right]^2 = 4\pi\left(\frac{3V}{4\pi}\right)^{\frac{2}{3}}$

$$= \frac{4\pi(3V)^{\frac{2}{3}}}{(4\pi)^{\frac{2}{3}}} = (3V)^{\frac{2}{3}} \times \frac{(4\pi)^1}{(4\pi)^{\frac{2}{3}}}$$

$$= (3V)^{\frac{2}{3}}(4\pi)^{1-\frac{2}{3}} = (4\pi)^{\frac{1}{3}}(3V)^{\frac{2}{3}}$$

Question 25: A

Let each unit length be x.

Thus, $S = 6x^2$. Therefore, $x = \left(\frac{S}{6}\right)^{\frac{1}{2}}$

$V = x^3$. Thus, $V = [\left(\frac{S}{6}\right)^{\frac{1}{2}}]^3$ so $V = \left(\frac{S}{6}\right)^{\frac{3}{2}}$

Question 26: B

Multiplying the second equation by 2 we get 4x + 16y = 24. Subtracting the first equation from this we get 13y = 17, so $y = \frac{17}{13}$. Then solving for x we get $x = \frac{10}{13}$. You could also try substituting possible solutions one by one, although given that the equations are both linear and contain easy numbers, it is quicker to solve them algebraically.

Question 27: A

Multiply by the denominator to give: $(7x + 10) = (3y^2 + 2)(9x + 5)$

Partially expand brackets on right side: $(7x + 10) = 9x(3y^2 + 2) + 5(3y^2 + 2)$

Take x terms across to left side: $7x - 9x(3y^2 + 2) = 5(3y^2 + 2) - 10$

Take x outside the brackets: $x[7 - 9(3y^2 + 2)] = 5(3y^2 + 2) - 10$

Thus: $x = \frac{5(3y^2 + 2) - 10}{7 - 9(3y^2 + 2)}$

Simplify to give: $x = \frac{(15y^2)}{(7 - 9(3y^2 + 2))}$

Question 28: F

$$3x\left(\frac{3x^7}{x^{\frac{1}{3}}}\right)^3 = 3x\left(\frac{3^3x^{21}}{x^{\frac{3}{3}}}\right)$$

$$= 3x\frac{27x^{21}}{x} = 81x^{21}$$

Question 29: D

$$2x[2^{\frac{7}{14}} x^{\frac{7}{14}}] = 2x[2^{\frac{1}{2}} x^{\frac{1}{2}}]$$

$$= 2x(\sqrt{2}\sqrt{x}) = 2\left[\sqrt{x}\sqrt{x}\right][\sqrt{2}\sqrt{x}]$$

$$= 2\sqrt{2x^3}$$

Question 30: A

$A = \pi r^2$, therefore $10\pi = \pi r^2$

Thus, $r = \sqrt{10}$

Therefore, the circumference is $2\pi\sqrt{10}$

Question 31: D

$3.4 = 12 + (3 + 4) = 19$

$19.5 = 95 + (19 + 5) = 119$

Question 32: D

$$2.3 = \frac{2^3}{2} = 4$$

$$4.2 = \frac{4^2}{4} = 4$$

Question 33: F
This is a tricky question that requires you to know how to 'complete the square':

$(x + 1.5)(x + 1.5) = x^2 + 3x + 2.25$

Thus, $(x + 1.5)^2 - 7.25 = x^2 + 3x - 5 = 0$

Therefore, $(x + 1.5)^2 = 7.25 = \frac{29}{4}$

Thus, $x + 1.5 = \sqrt{\frac{29}{4}}$

Thus $x = -\frac{3}{2} \pm \sqrt{\frac{29}{4}} = -\frac{3}{2} \pm \frac{\sqrt{29}}{2}$

Question 34: B
Whilst you definitely need to solve this graphically, it is necessary to complete the square for the first equation to allow you to draw it more easily:

$(x + 2)^2 = x^2 + 4x + 4$
Thus, $y = (x + 2)^2 + 10 = x^2 + 4x + 14$
This is now an easy curve to draw ($y = x^2$ that has moved 2 units left and 10 units up). The turning point of this quadratic is to the left and well above anything in x^3, so the only solution is the first intersection of the two curves in the upper right quadrant around (3.4, 39).

Question 35: C
By far the easiest way to solve this is to sketch them (don't waste time solving them algebraically). As soon as you've done this, it'll be very obvious that $y = 2$ and $y = 1-x^2$ don't intersect, since the latter has its turning point at (0, 1) and zero points at $x = -1$ and 1. $y = x$ and $y = x^2$ intersect at the origin and (1, 1), and $y = 2$ runs through both.

Question 36: B
Notice that you're not required to get the actual values – just the number's magnitude. Thus, 897653 can be approximated to 900,000 and 0.009764 to 0.01. Therefore, 900,000 x 0.01 = 9,000

Question 37: C

Multiply through by 70: $7(7x + 3) + 10(3x + 1) = 14 \times 70$

Simplify: $49x + 21 + 30x + 10 = 980$

$79x + 31 = 980$

$$x = \frac{949}{79}$$

Question 38: A

Split the equilateral triangle into 2 right-angled triangles and apply Pythagoras' theorem:

$$x^2 = \left(\frac{x}{2}\right)^2 + h^2 . \text{ Thus } h^2 = \frac{3}{4}x^2$$

$$h = \sqrt{\frac{3x^2}{4}} = \frac{\sqrt{3x^2}}{2}$$

The area of a triangle = $\frac{1}{2}$ x base x height $= \frac{1}{2}x\frac{\sqrt{3x^2}}{2}$

Simplifying gives: $x\frac{\sqrt{3x^2}}{4} = x\frac{\sqrt{3}\sqrt{x^2}}{4} = \frac{x^2\sqrt{3}}{4}$

Question 39: A

This is a question testing your ability to spot 'the difference between two squares'.

Factorise to give: $3 - \frac{7x(5x-1)(5x+1)}{(7x)^2(5x+1)}$

Cancel out: $3 - \frac{(5x-1)}{7x}$

Question 40: C

The easiest way to do this is to 'complete the square':

$(x - 5)^2 = x^2 - 10x + 25$

Thus, $(x - 5)^2 - 125 = x^2 - 10x - 100 = 0$

Therefore, $(x - 5)^2 = 125$

$x - 5 = \pm\sqrt{125} = \pm\sqrt{25}\sqrt{5} = \pm5\sqrt{5}$

$x = 5 \pm 5\sqrt{5}$

Question 41: B

Factorise by completing the square:

$x^2 - 4x + 7 = (x - 2)^2 + 3$

Simplify: $(x - 2)^2 = y^3 + 2 - 3$

$x - 2 = \pm\sqrt{y^3 - 1}$

$x = 2 \pm \sqrt{y^3 - 1}$

Question 42: D

Square both sides to give: $(3x + 2)^2 = 7x^2 + 2x + y$

Thus: $y = (3x + 2)^2 - 7x^2 - 2x = (9x^2 + 12x + 4) - 7x^2 - 2x$

$y = 2x^2 + 10x + 4$

Question 43: C

This is a fourth order polynomial, which you aren't expected to be able to factorise at GCSE. This is where looking at the options makes your life a lot easier. In all of them, opening the bracket on the right side involves making $(y \pm 1)^4$ on the left side, i.e. the answers are hinting that $(y \pm 1)^4$ is the solution to the fourth order polynomial.

Since there are negative terms in the equations (e.g. $-4y^3$), the solution has to be:

$(y-1)^4 = y^4 - 4y^3 + 6y^2 - 4y + 1$

Therefore, $(y-1)^4 + 1 = x^5 + 7$

Thus, $y - 1 = (x^5 + 6)^{\frac{1}{4}}$

$y = 1 + (x^5 + 6)^{1/4}$

Question 44: A

Let the width of the television be 4x and the height of the television be 3x.

Then by Pythagoras: $(4x)^2 + (3x)^2 = 50^2$

Simplify: $25x^2 = 2500$

Thus: $x = 10$. Therefore: the screen is **30 inches by 40 inches**, i.e. the area is 1,200 inches^2.

Question 45: C

Square both sides to give: $1 + \frac{3}{x^2} = (y^5 + 1)^2$

Multiply out: $\frac{3}{x^2} = (y^{10} + 2y^5 + 1) - 1$

Thus: $x^2 = \frac{3}{y^{10} + 2y^5}$

Therefore: $x = \sqrt{\frac{3}{y^{10} + 2y^5}}$

Question 46: C

The easiest way is to double the first equation and triple the second to get:
$6x - 10y = 20 \; and \; 6x + 6y = 39.$
Subtract the first from the second to give: $16y = 19$,
Therefore, $y = \frac{19}{16}$.
Substitute back into the first equation to give $x = \frac{85}{16}$.

Question 47: C

This is fairly straightforward; the first inequality is the easier one to work with: B and D and E violate it, so we just need to check A and C in the second inequality.

C: $1^3 - 2^2 < 3$, but A: $2^3 - 1^2 > 3$

Question 48: B

Whilst this can be done graphically, it's quicker to do algebraically (because the second equation is not as easy to sketch). Intersections occur where the curves have the same coordinates.

Thus: $x + 4 = 4x^2 + 5x + 5$

Simplify: $4x^2 + 4x + 1 = 0$

Factorise: $(2x + 1)(2x + 1) = 0$

Thus, the two graphs only intersect once at $x = -\dfrac{1}{2}$

Question 49: D

It's better to do this algebraically as the equations are easy to work with and you would need to sketch very accurately to get the answer. Intersections occur where the curves have the same coordinates. Thus: $x^3 = x$

$x^3 - x = 0$

Thus: $x(x^2 - 1) = 0$

Spot the 'difference between two squares': $x(x + 1)(x - 1) = 0$

Thus there are 3 intersections: at $x = 0, 1 \ and - 1$

Question 50: E

Note that the line is the hypotenuse of a right angled triangle with one side unit length and one side of length ½. By Pythagoras, $\left(\dfrac{1}{2}\right)^2 + 1^2 = x^2$

Thus, $x^2 = \dfrac{1}{4} + 1 = \dfrac{5}{4}$

$x = \sqrt{\dfrac{5}{4}} = \dfrac{\sqrt{5}}{\sqrt{4}} = \dfrac{\sqrt{5}}{2}$

Question 51: D

We can eliminate z from equation (1) and (2) by multiplying equation (1) by 3 and adding it to equation (2):

$3x + 3y - 3z = -3$	Equation (1) multiplied by 3
$\underline{2x - 2y + 3z = 8}$	Equation (2) then add both equations
$5x + y\quad = 5$	We label this as equation (4)

Now we must eliminate the same variable z from another pair of equations by using equation (1) and (3):

$2x + 2y - 2z = -2$	Equation (1) multiplied by 2
$\underline{2x - y + 2z = 9}$	Equation (3) then add both equations
$4x + y\quad = 7$	We label this as equation (5)

We now use both equations (4) and (5) to obtain the value of x:

$5x + y = 5$	Equation (4)
$\underline{-4x - y = -7}$	Equation (5) multiplied by -1
$x\quad = -2$	

Substitute x back in to calculate y:

$4x + y = 7$

$4(-2) + y = 7$

$-8 + y = 7$

$y = 15$

Substitute x and y back in to calculate z:

$x + y - z = -1$

$-2 + 15 - z = -1$

$13 - z = -1$

$-z = -14$

$z = 14$

Thus: $x = -2, y = 15, z = 14$

165

Question 52: D
This is one of the easier maths questions. Take 3a as a factor to give:

$3a(a^2 - 10a + 25)$ $= 3a(a - 5)(a - 5) = 3a(a - 5)^2$

Question 53: B
Note that 12 is the Lowest Common Multiple of 3 and 4. Thus:

-3 (4x + 3y) = -3 (48)   Multiply each side by -3

4 (3x + 2y) = 4 (34)   Multiply each side by 4

-12x − 9y = -144

$\underline{12x + 8y = 136}$ Add together

    -y = -8

    y = 8

Substitute y back in: 4x + 3y = 48

4x + 3(8) = 48

4x + 24 = 48

4x = 24

x = 6

Question 54: E
Don't be fooled, this is an easy question, just obey BODMAS and don't skip steps.

$$\frac{-(25-28)^2}{-36+14} = \frac{-(-3)^2}{-22}$$

This gives: $\frac{-(9)}{-22} = \frac{9}{22}$

Question 55: E
Since there are 26 possible letters for each of the 3 letters in the license plate, and there are 10 possible numbers (0-9) for each of the 3 numbers in the same plate, then the number of license plates would be:

$(26) \times (26) \times (26) \times (10) \times (10) \times (10) = 17,576,000$

Question 56: B

Expand the brackets to give: $4x^2 - 12x + 9 = 0$.

Factorise: $(2x - 3)(2x - 3) = 0$.

Thus, only one solution exists, x = 1.5.

Note that you could also use the fact that the discriminant, $b^2 - 4ac = 0$ to get the answer.

Question 57: C

$$= \left(x^{\frac{1}{2}}\right)^{\frac{1}{2}} (y^{-3})^{\frac{1}{2}}$$

$$= x^{\frac{1}{4}} y^{-\frac{3}{2}} = \frac{x^{\frac{1}{4}}}{y^{\frac{3}{2}}}$$

Question 58: A

Let x, y, and z represent the rent for the 1-bedroom, 2-bedroom, and 3-bedroom flats, respectively. We can write 3 different equations: 1 for the rent, 1 for the repairs, and the last one for the statement that the 3-bedroom unit costs twice as much as the 1-bedroom unit.

(1) x + y + z = 1240

(2) 0.1x + 0.2y + 0.3z = 276

(3) z = 2x

Substitute z = 2x in both of the two other equations to eliminate z:

(4) x + y + 2x = 3x + y = 1240

(5) 0.1x + 0.2y + 0.3(2x) = 0.7x + 0.2y = 276

-2(3x + y) = -2(1240)   Multiply each side of (4) by -2

10(0.7x + 0.2y) = 10(276)   Multiply each side of (5) by 10

(6) -6x -2y = -2480   Add these 2 equations

167

(7) 7x + 2y = 2760

x = 280

z = 2(280) = 560   Because z = 2x

280 + y + 560 = 1240   Because x + y + z = 1240

y = 400

Thus the units rent for £ 280, £ 400, £ 560 per week respectively.

Question 59: C
Following BODMAS:

$$= 5 \left[5(6^2 - 5 \times 3) + 400^{\frac{1}{2}}\right]^{1/3} + 7$$

$$= 5 \left[5(36 - 15) + 20\right]^{\frac{1}{3}} + 7$$

$$= 5 \left[5(21) + 20\right]^{\frac{1}{3}} + 7$$

$$= 5 \left(105 + 20\right)^{\frac{1}{3}} + 7$$

$$= 5 \left(125\right)^{\frac{1}{3}} + 7$$

$$= 5 (5) + 7$$

$$= 25 + 7 = 32$$

Question 60: B

Consider a triangle formed by joining the centre to two adjacent vertices. Six similar triangles can be made around the centre – thus, the central angle is 60 degrees. Since the two lines forming the triangle are of equal length, we have 6 identical equilateral triangles in the hexagon.

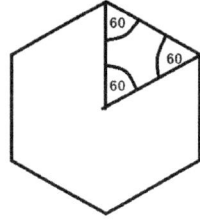

Now split the triangle in half and apply Pythagoras' theorem:

$$1^2 = 0.5^2 + h^2$$

Thus, $h = \sqrt{\frac{3}{4}} = \frac{\sqrt{3}}{2}$

Thus, the area of the triangle is: $\frac{1}{2}bh = \frac{1}{2} \times 1 \times \frac{\sqrt{3}}{2} = \frac{\sqrt{3}}{4}$

Therefore, the area of the hexagon is: $\frac{\sqrt{3}}{4} \times 6 = \frac{3\sqrt{3}}{2}$

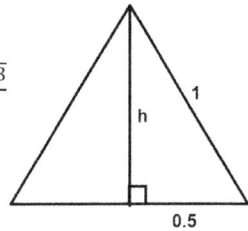

Question 61: B

Let x be the width and x+19 be the length.

Thus, the area of a rectangle is x(x + 19) = 780.

Therefore:

$x^2 + 19x - 780 = 0$

(x - 20)(x + 39) = 0

x – 20 = 0 or x + 39 = 0

x = 20 or x = -39

Since length can never be a negative number, we disregard x = -39 and use x = 20 instead.

Thus, the width is 20 metres and the length is 39 metres.

Question 62: B

The quickest way to solve is by trial and error, substituting the provided options. However, if you're keen to do this algebraically, you can do the following:

Start by setting up the equations: Perimeter = 2L + 2W = 34

Thus: L + W = 17

Using Pythagoras: $L^2 + W^2 = 13^2$

Since L + W = 17, W = 17 - L

Therefore: $L^2 + (17 - L)^2 = 169$

$L^2 + 289 - 34L + L^2 = 169$

$2L^2 - 34L + 120 = 0$

$L^2 - 17L + 60 = 0$

$(L - 5) (L - 12) = 0$

Thus: L = 5 and L = 12

And: W = 12 and W = 5

Question 63: C

Multiply both sides by 8: $4(3x - 5) + 2(x + 5) = 8(x + 1)$
Remove brackets: $\quad 12x - 20 + 2x + 10 = 8x + 8$
Simplify: $\quad 14x - 10 = 8x + 8$
Add 10: $\quad 14x = 8x + 18$
Subtract 8x: $\quad 6x = 18$
Therefore: $\quad x = 3$

Question 64: C

Recognise that 1.742 x 3 is 5.226. Now, the original equation simplifies to: $=$
$\dfrac{3 \times 10^6 + 3 \times 10^5}{10^{10}}$

$= 3 \times 10^{-4} + 3 \times 10^{-5} = 3.3 \times 10^{-4}$

Question 65: A

$$Area = \frac{(2+\sqrt{2})(4-\sqrt{2})}{2}$$

$$= \frac{8 - 2\sqrt{2} + 4\sqrt{2} - 2}{2}$$

$$= \frac{6 + 2\sqrt{2}}{2}$$

$$= 3 + \sqrt{2}$$

Question 66: C

Square both sides: $\frac{4}{x} + 9 = (y-2)^2$

$$\frac{4}{x} = (y-2)^2 - 9$$

Cross Multiply: $\frac{x}{4} = \frac{1}{(y-2)^2 - 9}$

$$x = \frac{4}{y^2 - 4y + 4 - 9}$$

Factorise: $x = \frac{4}{y^2 - 4y - 5}$

$$x = \frac{4}{(y+1)(y-5)}$$

Question 67: D

Set up the equation: $5x - 5 = 0.5(6x + 2)$

$$10x - 10 = 6x + 2$$

$$4x = 12$$

$$x = 3$$

Question 68: C

Round numbers appropriately: $\frac{55 + (\frac{9}{4})^2}{\sqrt{900}} = \frac{55 + \frac{81}{16}}{30}$

81 rounds to 80 to give: $\frac{55 + 5}{30} = \frac{60}{30} = 2$

Question 69: D

There are three outcomes from choosing the type of cheese in the crust. For each of the additional toppings to possibly add, there are 2 outcomes: 1 to include and another not to include a certain topping, for each of the 7 toppings

Thus, the number of different kinds of pizza is: $3 \times 2 \times 2 \times 2 \times 2 \times 2 \times 2 \times 2 = 3 \times 2^7$

$= 3 \times 128 = 384$

Question 70: A

Although it is possible to do this algebraically, by far the easiest way is via trial and error. The clue that you shouldn't attempt it algebraically is the fact that rearranging the first equation to make x or y the subject leaves you with a difficult equation to work with (e.g. $x = \sqrt{1 - y^2}$) when you try to substitute in the second.

An exceptionally good student might notice that the equations are symmetric in x and y, i.e. the solution is when x = y. Thus $2x^2 = 1$ and $2x = \sqrt{2}$ which gives $\frac{\sqrt{2}}{2}$ as the answer.

Question 71: C

If two shapes are congruent, then they are the same size and shape. Thus, congruent objects can be rotations and mirror images of each other. The two triangles in E are indeed congruent (SAS). Congruent objects must, by definition, have the same angles.

Question 72: B

Rearrange the equation: $x^2 + x - 6 \geq 0$

Factorise: $(x + 3)(x - 2) \geq 0$

Remember that this is a quadratic inequality so requires a quick sketch to ensure you don't make a silly mistake with which way the sign is.

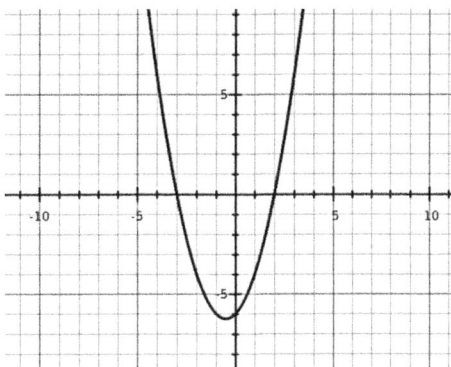

Thus, $y = 0$ when $x = 2$ and $x = -3$. $y > 0$ when $x > 2$ or $x < -3$.

Thus, the solution is: $x \leq -3 \, and \, x \geq 2$.

Question 73: B

Using Pythagoras: $a^2 + b^2 = x^2$

Since the triangle is isosceles: $a = b, so \, 2a^2 = x^2$

Area $= \frac{1}{2} base \, x \, height = \frac{1}{2} a^2$. From above, $a^2 = \frac{x^2}{2}$

Thus the area $= \frac{1}{2} x \frac{x^2}{2} = \frac{x^2}{4}$

Question 74: A

If X and Y are doubled, the value of Q increases by 4. Halving the value of A reduces this to 2. Finally, tripling the value of B reduces this to ⅔, i.e. the value decreases by ⅓.

Question 75: C

The quickest way to do this is to sketch the curves. This requires you to factorise both equations by completing the square:

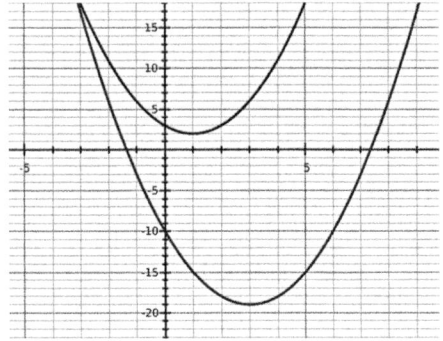

$$x^2 - 2x + 3 = (x - 1)^2 + 2$$

$$x^2 - 6x - 10 = (x - 3)^2 - 19$$

Thus, the first equation has a turning point at (1, 2) and doesn't cross the x-axis.

The second equation has a turning point at (3, -19) and crosses the x-axis twice.

FINAL ADVICE

Arrive well rested, well fed and well hydrated

The NBT is an intensive test, so make sure you're ready for it. Ensure you get a good night's sleep before the exam (there is little point cramming) and don't miss breakfast. If you're taking water into the exam then make sure you've been to the toilet before so you don't have to leave during the exam. Make sure you're well rested and fed to be at your best!

Move on

If you're struggling, move on. Every question has equal weighting and there is no negative marking. In the time it takes to answer on hard question, you could gain three times the marks by answering the easier ones. Be smart to score points- especially in section 2 where some questions are far easier than others.

Afterword

Remember that the route to a high score is your approach and practice. Don't fall into the trap that *"you can't prepare for the NBT"*– this could not be further from the truth. With knowledge of the test, some useful time-saving techniques and plenty of practice you can dramatically boost your score.

Work hard, never give up and do yourself justice.

Good luck!

Acknowledgements

I would like to express my sincerest thanks to the many people who helped make this book possible, especially the tutors who shared their expertise in compiling the huge number of questions and answers.

Rohan

ABOUT US

We currently publish over 85 titles across a range of subject areas – covering specialised admissions tests, examination techniques, personal statement guides, plus everything else you need to improve your chances of getting on to competitive courses such as medicine and law, as well as into universities such as Oxford and Cambridge.

Outside of publishing we also operate a highly successful tuition division, called UniAdmissions. This company was founded in 2013 by Dr Rohan Agarwal and Dr David Salt, both Cambridge Medical graduates with several years of tutoring experience. Since then, every year, hundreds of applicants and schools work with us on our programmes. Through the programmes we offer, we deliver expert tuition, exclusive course places, online courses, best-selling textbooks and much more.

With a team of over 1,000 Oxbridge tutors and a proven track record, UniAdmissions have quickly become the UK's number one admissions company.

Visit and engage with us at:

Website (UniAdmissions): www.uniadmissions.co.uk

Facebook: www.facebook.com/uniadmissionsuk

YOUR FREE BOOK

Thanks for purchasing this Ultimate Book. Readers like you have the power to make or break a book —hopefully you found this one useful and informative. *UniAdmissions* would love to hear about your experiences with this book. As thanks for your time we'll send you another ebook from our Ultimate Guide series absolutely <u>FREE</u>!

How to Redeem Your Free Ebook

1) Find the book you have on your Amazon purchase history or your email receipt to help find the book on Amazon.

2) On the product page at the Customer Reviews area, click 'Write a customer review'. Write your review and post it! Copy the review page or take a screen shot of the review you have left.

3) Head over to www.uniadmissions.co.uk/free-book and select your chosen free ebook!

Your ebook will then be emailed to you – it's as simple as that!

Alternatively, you can buy all the titles at

<u>www.uniadmissions.co.uk</u>

Printed in Great Britain
by Amazon